# INTEGRITY SWITCH

## A GUIDE FOR ASPIRING, DEVELOPING, AND EMERGING LEADERS

To book Joel Dearing as a speaker, presenter,
or for a leadership training program for an
athletic team or business,
visit: www.dearingleadership.com
or email: dearingleadership@gmail.com

Cover and Illustrations by Sean Cooney
Interior Design by NRK Designs

ISBN: 979-8-9900808-0-5
First Edition

Published by Dearing Leadership
Florida

# INTEGRITY SWITCH

## A GUIDE FOR ASPIRING, DEVELOPING, AND EMERGING LEADERS

By
Joel B. Dearing

Florida

OTHER BOOKS BY JOEL B. DEARING

*Volleyball Fundamentals*
(1st edition, 2003)
( 2nd edition, 2019)

*The Untold Story of William G. Morgan - Inventor of Volleyball*
*2007*

PUBLISHED ARTICLES

*Follow The Leader: Beyond Captain Selection.*
Coaching Volleyball.

*Rally Scoring For Every Deciding Game*
Coaching Volleyball.

*Combination Drills* (with Lev Milman, co-author),
Scholastic Coach.

*Bonusball.*
Coaching Volleyball.

# Dedication

This book is dedicated to my father, David B. Dearing. Shooting baskets with my Dad is one of my most vivid memories from my childhood. I can still picture that first basket. A wooden backboard nailed to a large circular pole—this was the first of several baskets in front of which I would spend hours. I just loved the feel of a swish or the ever-reliable bank shot. Dad made a lot of those.

In my early years, Dad was a coach and I loved watching him at his craft. He was my first youth basketball coach, and I loved every minute of that season. I will never forget my first trip with him to the tourney at the Bangor Auditorium. We watched several quarter-final match-ups of eastern Maine high school teams we had never seen play. As each game went on, he spied qualities in certain players and pointed them out to me.

He also started telling me story after story of high school coaching seasons starting back before I came along. I knew early on that I was going to be a coach. His influence over time as he moved into educational administration, expanded as I took one leadership lesson after another from our many conversations. I soaked them all up. One by one, his perspectives on effective coaching and leadership approaches became ingrained to this day:

- There is no substitute for preparation —"never try to execute what hasn't been practiced".

- Expect the unexpected.
- Give each kid their chance, their opportunity.
- Planning paves the way for success—plan the work, then work the plan.

Of the principles that emerged, some became part of my leadership DNA from osmosis, including my favorite that I refer to as "that's your shot". The whole idea of instilling self-confidence in athletes was one of his hallmarks. Among other things as a leader, Dad was a master psychologist. He utilized this as a parent (and grand-parent), as a coach, teacher, educational administrator, leader, and leader of leaders.

No observations about Dad would be complete without mentioning my mom, Doris, and their 57 years together. Their devotion and commitment to each other, and their children provided a great example to follow. Not surprisingly, my siblings Joy, Dan, Jonathan, and I all followed in his footsteps with careers in education. At last count, our collective tally in adding to his legacy is well over 100 years.

I think you'll enjoy getting to know my Dad much better as you read along.

# Acknowledgments

Thank you to my wife, Diane. Unlike a few previous writing projects with tight deadlines, and start to finish productivity—this one took "years". You must have secretly thumbed through the full draft on the dining room table at least once, to ensure every page was not filled with, "All work and no play makes Jack a dull boy".

A special thanks to my daughter, Erin Rosario and her business partner, Julie Duff, and their team at www.roseandgold.com for the ongoing marketing and promotion of my business and this book. An extra thanks to Erin for serving as one of my readers of the first full draft. Thanks as well to three former students and emerging leaders, Kelsey Armstrong, Ryan Coale, and Colleen O'Connell, who also provided lots of feedback as first draft readers.

Tributes to Dad and Mom have been taken care of in the book dedication. To my sons, Kevin and Ryan, lessons and insights I am learning from both of you in your professional careers are included in here. I'm sure you will smile when you come across them.

A heartfelt thanks to my friend and brother, Marcus Jannitto, for providing the Foreword, lots of feedback on the drafts, and for decades of leadership collaboration. You are an inspiration to so many, and your impact on leaders will be felt for generations. I thoroughly enjoyed working with Sean Cooney and his team at DG Graphics. Somehow, they took my simple image sketches and created final products that topped my imagination.

To my friend and fellow author and leadership collaborator, Paul Thornton, thank you for sharing suggestions from your experiences in publishing through Amazon, and connecting me to Nick Caya. Nick, thank you for the many prompt responses as my Word-2-Kindle book guide.

To every client and customer of Dearing Leadership, LLC. who has given me business and the opportunity to develop my craft in providing seminars, workshops, and motivational talks—thank you! Much of the content of this book represents the work done there, and I am grateful for your support.

My thanks also go out to Gerry and Lorry Hausman for their expertise as manuscript advisors. Your insight and advice in reviewing the early draft was most helpful. A special thank you to Nancy Koucky for taking charge of all aspects of the book design and getting me to the finish line. Your expertise and attention to detail was superb.

Literally, hundreds of names and faces of former coaches, teachers, leaders, players, students, colleagues, friends, and family have come to my mind over the many years of pulling this book together. Many of you are referred to in the stories shared. Especially to each one reading this who knows me, thank you for supporting me in getting your own copy of this book, and for your impact in my own leadership development.

A final thought that has meaning to me from Colossians 3:23. "Whatever you do, work at it with all your heart, as though you were working for The Lord, and not for people."[1] I do thank The Lord for the many years of guiding my work.

# Table of Contents

# Foreword

There are times.

Our call sign was Rhody 23. We had just taken off in our C-130 from Pope AFB in North Carolina, on a simulated combat mission to resupply friendly ground forces at a forward operating base (FOB). The 14-day exercise ran 24/7 and involved more than 28 aircraft and almost 1,000 USAF and Army personnel. On the ground in the exercise area were "red" team members, the bad guys whose job it was to engage and shoot down our aircraft using simulated SAMs (surface to air missiles) We had a 'referee' on board, an Air Force Lt Colonel instructor pilot (IP) that would 'kill' us if we flew too close to the red SAM teams on the ground, or if he determined that our tactics and evasive maneuvers were not sufficiently aggressive enough to prevent a shoot down.

I was the navigator on the crew of six, and the person who had to ensure we not only avoided threats along the route, but that we would be on time (+- 30 secs) and positioned in an exact spot in the sky that would carry our air dropped loads into the center of the 400 x 400 yard drop zone (DZ). Of course, timing is everything. The red teams knew exactly what time we would be overhead at any given point in our route, giving them a distinct advantage. As we sat on the ground waiting for takeoff clearance, I asked ground control to clear us for departure 4 minutes prior to our scheduled time. They initially balked but gave us the early takeoff. To mitigate the threat, we gamed it: we had planned to fly the route 20 kts faster than the flight plan called for, which put us over each checkpoint on our 300ft low-level route several minutes early, hopefully before the bad guys expected us.

As we ran the Combat Entry checklist our referee looked at me and said, "You know you're gonna be early, right?" I said "Yep". "Like 5 minutes early". I said "Exactly 5 minutes early". He looked at me like I had 2 heads. In combat airlift the idea is to be on time on target. If we're early, our troops on the ground may not be at the drop zone or ready to defend it. If we're late, we could expose them to a threat for a potentially deadly amount of time. Flying faster and being earlier than expected would minimize the ground threat, but potentially had us lingering in the hostile DZ area until our planned drop time.

As we flew the route all indications were that we caught the red teams off-guard by being early. As usual with this type of mission, we were horsing that big airplane around hills and down valleys at 5 miles per minute. As we hit our last checkpoint and were lining up for our slowdown and lineup for the DZ, we diverged to the north about 4 miles off course and initiated a standard-rate 4 minute 360-degree turn. We started our slowdown as we headed back to the DZ lineup for our drop, now on time. The ref came in the intercom and said "You can't do a 360 in the combat area!"and was ready to call a "no-drop" and send us home.

There are times.

There are times when you press the rules to the edge and let the refs sort it out. There are times when your sole purpose is to get your teammates the things they need to stay in the fight and thrive in spite of your own needs. There are times when you spend so much time out of the box that you have to redraw it. There are times when the season is getting long, your team is battle weary and motivation is low; times when conflicts loom, blind spots become visible and mistakes from the past are dragging us down. What do you do?

This book is about those times.

There are times when we have to have the courage, willingness and imagination to try things, to see things differently; to reframe and adjust our approach to traditional team issues of communication, failure, trust (and trustworthiness), unclear roles and fading motivation.

There are times, as Joel talks about, when coaches and teammates need to visibly embrace one of the most important attributes of a great leader: curiosity. Being curious causes you to ask the right questions during those hard conversations, or to always listen like the other person's words are the most important thing in the world. Being curious means approaching each day at work with the question "What if…" and to wonder enough about what you don't know to realize that you have some blind spots that others can help you fill in.…and there are simply times when you have to stand in the gap.

If you have been a coach or supervisor for any length of time, this book will be a familiar place. Joel leans heavily on illustrations, examples and stories of people who have affected how he coached, led and thought during his 40+ seasons. He would be the first to tell you that he "never had an original idea in his life", but I would argue that his framework of directionality ("BELOW" – "BEHIND" – "ABOVE" and "AHEAD") uniquely allows the reader to enter the conversation anywhere that strikes them, and that his idea of the Integrity Switch and leadership scales give us a GPS location of where we are and where we can go with our conversations, our response to failure, feedback, change, team commitment and my favorite: the "to do" scale. As you will, I constantly found myself rewriting parts of these scales to fit my style and situation, which is Joel's intent.

This book is not a prescription for leadership; it's a self-guided tour filled with stories and examples of things that did work well and some that did not. For the younger coach especially, Joel presents the opportunity to tap into the wisdom of a very successful coaching career, not only by sharing what worked for him but by giving you the tools to build your own solution.

For those of us who have done it for most of our lives, there are times where we can see clearly the magic of coaching and of sport: to have a chance to change the world and influence the next generation one conversation, one situation, one player and one game at a time. This book is about those times. I hope you learn as much as I did.

Marcus Jannitto
USAF Brigadier General (ret)
Navigator, Coach, Dad

I'm not sure if I can have an Epilogue within a Foreword, but I read Joel's book, so here it is anyway: I was sitting in the casual bar at Pope that night having a beer with the crew, and our ref sits down next to me. We had hit the DZ 3 seconds early, made our drop of 'beans and bullets' to the friendly forces on the ground and successfully evaded back to the base. We flew one more mission that day with the same ref and a similar result, but without the intentional 360.

He said "You were lucky today: your 360 was in an area where there was no threat." I said "It wasn't luck Sir – we got good intel and knew that area was relatively safe." He said "It won't work every time." I said "I know, but it worked today." He nodded "It worked today." He bought me a fresh beer and went on "…but you know Captain, there are times…"

# Preface: *A²B² Leadership*

Only in the process of working on this book, have I come to fully understand *my four primary objectives* for getting it published:

- to help aspiring, developing, and emerging leaders and others in leadership.
- to get all the leadership training and team building ideas and program content I use in my leadership business collected and available for the benefit of others.
- to share the leadership framework that I have developed.
- to pay tribute to and honor my father.

This preface has two significant purposes to set the stage for all that will follow:

- to share the origin of the book title
- to define and describe the *A²B² Leadership* framework that I have developed.

## The Origin of "Integrity Switch"

The professor arrived early for the first class of the semester, and knew the graduate students filtering in would be expecting the *same old song and dance*. After all, having advanced through one college degree already, they knew the drill. By now on the first day of a new course, they had grown accustomed to enduring the course architect at the front of the room delivering some type of statement about the importance of the course. This would typically be followed by the obligatory syllabus review highlighted with the standard reminders about plagiarism and academic honesty.

Of note this day, appearing to be intentionally and prominently hanging from the top of the white board at the front of the room, were two graduation gowns. The professor greeted the gathered scholars with an announcement, "The course syllabus is now available to you through our online platform. Please review it prior to our next class meeting, and I will entertain any and all related questions you have at that time."

He walked over and pulled a graduation gown off the hanger, began to pull it on, and then made this request, "I'm looking for a volunteer to play the role of our college president in a one-act play". Not expecting an immediate response, he zipped up his robe, grabbed what appeared to be a white tube wrapped up with a ribbon, and while holding that aloft, he added, "You get to present me with my diploma". Eventually, a hand went up, and the professor handed both the diploma and the other gown to the volunteer. "Now, here are your directions", the professor offered to the student, "hold that tube in your left hand, and when I point at you, simply call my name loudly, and when I arrive next to you, place the tube in my left hand, then shake my right hand and hold that pose for the photo".

The Professor paused, then looked at the room full of students and asked them to grab their cell phones. "Here is your part", the professor shared with the group. "Before we begin, I need you to search what percentage of college students report anonymously that they cheat. Go ahead and shout out the percentage you discover". After a brief, but awkward pause, numbers ranging from 60 to 90 started filling the air, until eventually one student said, "86 percent". The professor held up a hand and added, "that is the number I found when I did that search". He grabbed a piece of posterboard with a string attached, placed it around his neck, so everyone could see a very large 86% displayed. The professor then said, "We are almost ready to begin, and this will be a very short play. I represent 86% of you who cheat despite having made the decision to pursue leadership as a career". He went on to inform the group, that he would have only one line in this play, delivered to conclude that act. "Once I do that", the professor stated, "we will show appreciation to our volunteer president, and then resume our class together, and I am going to ask you to pair up and discuss a simple question".

With that, the professor pointed at the *robed president*, who right on cue, loudly announced his name. The *graduate* moved energetically to join the president, and beamed at the crowd during the pose. He began to stride away holding the prize now in his possession high, and looking out in the direction of those in attendance who had supported his noble efforts. Suddenly, the graduate halted his gait, took a deep breath and exhaled slowly and fully. With great optimism and a clear sigh of relief, he delivered the big line, arguably a big lie, "Now. . . I can live an honest life", and triumphantly strode off the stage.

Back to reality, after pausing intentionally for several seconds, the Professor then unzipped the robe, placed it back on the hanger, dropped the diploma prop back on a desk, and invited applause for the student who played the part of the President. Allowing some time for it all to sink in, the Professor eventually stepped back into that role. "So, let me get this straight. Is that how it works? We engage and practice dishonesty for years, and then all of a sudden we go into the world, into the workplace, and we will bring integrity to that". Pausing for effect, he continued, "Is that really how it works?" That is your discussion question. Eventually, the classroom discussion turned lively as everyone began chiming in with their thoughts.

The Professor brought the class to a close with this final thought, "Let your most recent venture in academic dishonesty be your last one. Start today in this class, and raise the standard for yourself. Flip your *integrity switch* on today. Keep it on throughout this and your other courses, and see if you don't begin to feel a little better about yourself. Stand tall with the 14% that appear to be out there, who recognize that the key to living and working with honesty and integrity is to practice it daily. Envision the day in the not-too-distant future when you walk across the stage and pose with our President as you receive your diploma. Choose now to walk off that stage with your integrity intact, well-rehearsed, and ready for the daily challenges you will encounter in building your professional reputation. Class dismissed."

Ever get tired of hearing yourself speak in a leadership role? Have you found yourself in the *front of the room* delivering messages, and noticed the recipients shifting in their seats with eyes glossed over? Despite being a seasoned professor, somewhere along the line, I had that feeling as I reviewed the course syllabus on day one with some very sharp students. Instead of my own voice, all I could hear in my head was Miss Othmar's, "Wah wah WAH wah" as depicted in Charlie Brown's classroom scenes. I vowed never again, and went to work on the one-act play, described above that I presented the following semester, and eventually titled, *Integrity Switch*.

I enjoyed all the debriefs with future students who took part in that play. Eventually, I turned it into an activity during leadership workshops and seminars, as a way of introducing the all-important topic of integrity. Sometimes, we need help as emerging leaders to catch a vision of and for ourselves. To this day, a month does not go by in hearing from one of my students looking for some advice. Often the conversation circles around to the benefit they have derived from personalizing the *integrity switch* message.

So, the challenge is to flip on that switch and keep it blazing. Sounds good, but, what if ____ ? Sure, fill in the blank. Our minds and our plans change all the time. With full integrity over the years, I have eagerly committed to a morning foursome. A tweaky back, hip, or shoulder has led to more than one cancellation. I never enjoyed making that decision, but it was not lacking integrity. Unforeseen circumstances will cause changes in commitments and decisions for you too, and those situations may place your reputation on the line in someone else's eyes. As you take on leadership opportunities, you will gain experience handling uncomfortable moments. Do your best to respond directly and honestly to each challenge you face, and you will learn valuable lessons from each one.

In creating a one-act play, the phrase, "integrity switch" became a significant leadership principle for me, and an easy choice as the book title. We will jump right back into the topic of integrity in Chapter One.

# Development of the
# $A^2B^2$ Leadership Framework

It was the summer of 2008, and in my typical August fashion, summer jogs through the running trails right behind our home, became season theme hunting excursions. The "Begin with the end in mind" concept had become a part of me by this time. Popularized by Stephen Covey as one of the 7 habits of highly effective leaders,[2] the applications of this phrase available to benefit a leader or an organization are endless.

I was on a mission to begin the upcoming season with a powerful stepping off point. I had lots of daily jogging routes available, from narrow ways lined with saplings to rolling hills with hard packed paths—some hidden in the forest, and others in open landscape. Regardless of the circuitous trip I generally determined in advance, every tour began on a pine needle trail that started with a straightaway just about 120 running steps long. Not a good sign that I know that!

On this particular day as I rounded that first corner, my mind was somewhere else. A handful of face first plunges over the years, initiated by an unfortunate union of my shoe meeting one of the many roots on the trail, taught me to think and scan ahead at the same time. I remember reflecting on the work accomplished in the off-season with a couple of devoted captains. I began thinking about the direction we needed in our program and specifically for the upcoming season. This idea brought arrows to mind, since they are a common symbol to use in marking out directions.

Over a matter of a few days, a vision for combining a number of arrows in a helpful pattern went on a piece of paper. I loved the idea immediately. This idea of turning the direction of arrows into a season theme became more powerful for me over those final days of summer. As pre-season approached, the image below depicts where I intended to confidently lead this group.

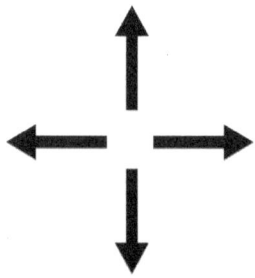

In between one of our double session days, I set time aside for a team building activity. I recall splitting the team up into small groups. I provided each group with a posterboard, tape, and four big arrows, each one filling a full sheet of paper. I sent them off with instructions to "Arrange and place your arrows on the poster in a way that creates a powerful theme that could be useful to the team". All of this is how I remember it, which does not mean it is all accurate, but the impact of how this played out is completely true.

I expected these small groups to return with different arrangements of these symbols. My plan was to ask each sub group to share their illustrated theme, and then. . . reveal mine. Armed with inspiration from their coach, reflected by a powerful model that I was certain they would endorse, the season would begin. Somehow, they too were inspired by this simple activity. The players came back, but the activity took a life of its' own. Synergy from among might be better than energy from one, even if that individual is the one in charge. Leaders learn this.

The team was brimming with confidence. By brimming, I mean grinning ear to ear, eyes alive, joy erupting confidence. Apparently, not waiting for further instructions, the groups compared notes, and collectively agreed on a model. Someone announced with total glee, "Coach, we got it!", and revealed the array of arrows depicted below.

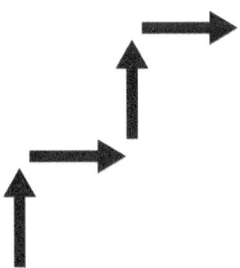

The collaborative effort produced a one step at a time theme, with the arrows arranged to simulate steps. Hard to push back on that notion. What coach would not love to know players were staying in the moment, not getting ahead of themselves, or dwelling on the past. So, I did what any sensible coach would have done. Leaning into a very limited acting career back in my primary grades, I pasted an ear-to-ear grin on my face. My response was a fist-pumping, depth of my soul triumphant exclamation of "You got it"! I learned so many lessons about leadership from my teams. We talk about all being on the same page, and in this case, it was critical that I jumped onto their page. Throughout that very successful season, those players worked diligently to stay in the moment. They continued to develop their model by defining the steps that would lead them to success.

I did not let go of the formation of arrows I had in mind for that team. I began to develop it into a leadership framework. I chose four simple words to bring definition to the direction of each arrow.

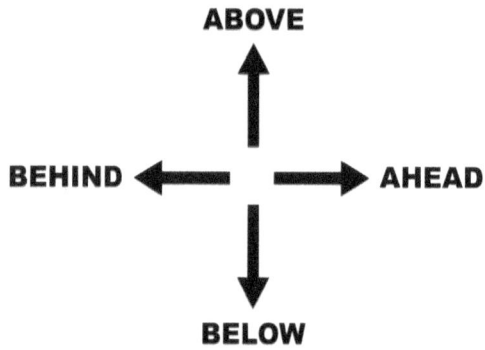

Over time, I developed lessons representing leadership topics, issues, and challenges that could relate to these two "A" words, and two "B" words. Eventually those words inspired the idea of a book with four related sections, and in that process, a name emerged: *A²B² Leadership* represents my leadership development framework. Deciding on the sequence to reveal the four arrows, and eventually arrange in the Table of Contents took some time.

**A² = AHEAD & ABOVE.** Should I come out of the starting blocks with these two perspectives? After all, just as an effective lead-off batter gets the full attention of the starting pitcher, so too might a powerful stepping off point capture your attention. Having a vision fits nicely with looking AHEAD while *rising or reaching* are concepts easily relatable to ABOVE.

**B$^2$ = BEHIND & BELOW**. One can easily argue that these two terms are no less powerful and equally essential perspectives. A thoughtful look back provides lots of life lessons to build upon from experiences now BEHIND us. I will readily admit that the over-used challenge question, "How is that working out for you?", started getting annoying to me some years ago. The concept however, is useful should we use it to guide some reflective thinking. The idea of BELOW obviously brings a strong foundation and core values to mind. Identifying and clarifying a mission statement, along with clearly establishing the non-negotiables that will be reflected in your culture, fit here as well.

When I finally settled on twelve-chapter topics to disperse in the four sections, I kept asking myself one question, "Where should I begin?" My favorite Tom Peters phrase is "The blinding flash of the obvious"[3], and eventually I did have the "Aha" moment in making that decision. Hoping to include "Begin with the end in mind" in a visual framework for *A$^2$B$^2$ Leadership* eventually led to the decision to begin with BELOW and unwrap in a clockwise fashion by then looking BEHIND and ABOVE. The final destination lies AHEAD and will emerge as you follow along.

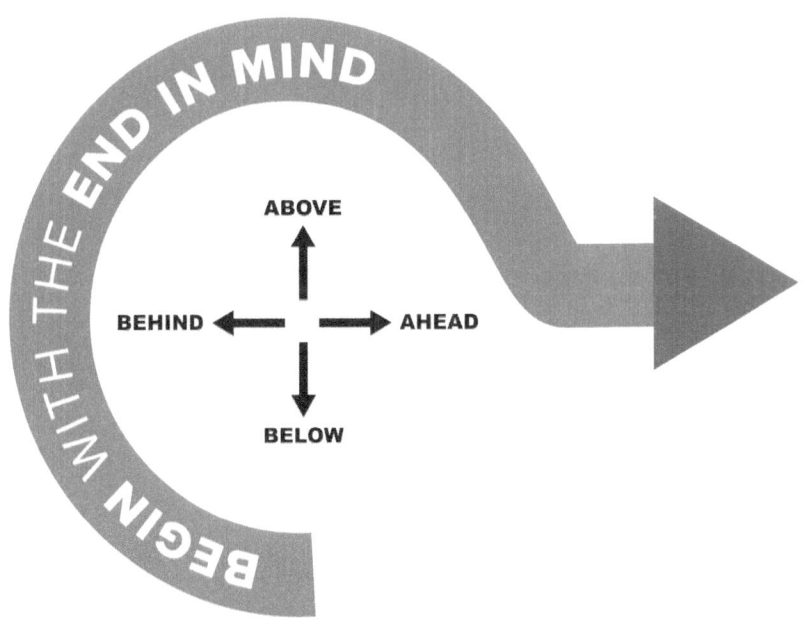

The hope is that you find at least one page to stick a bookmark into, because the content made you pause or mark with a star, perhaps even write a note in the margin. For those accessing on a device, I would encourage you to grab a notebook to jot down notes or take on activities that will be presented, especially in the chapter review sections.

I wondered at times when I would cross the final "t" and dot the last "i". Throughout all the drafts, I had others in mind. Countless leaders invested in me, modeled leadership in front of me, and guided me over the years. My opportunities to lead, and the related responsibilities, inspired me in fulfilling a core value of *helping others*. As you explore the content, *I hope something you discover helps you.*

# Introduction – Leadership Scales

*" If you know what makes sense and what is nonsense, and you can separate the best way to do something from the easy way, you'll probably come out all right most of the time ".*

This quote represents a hidden gem in a letter from my Dad. The *easy way* versus the *best way*. Sage advice for leaders certainly, and what a great way to frame the topic of how best *to do*, or *to handle* something. I re-discovered this letter that I had kept for decades in the early months of mourning the loss of this influential leader and most loving father. Within days, I added his quote to my signature page template that I used for work related communication, and placed his name at the end. This tribute reminded me daily that leaders must develop independent thinking to effectively frame issues, challenges, and obstacles.

I began to share this message in leadership training sessions. In one session I used a Likert scale style to display the key elements. Are you familiar with this type of scale? They are often used in a research study or routinely when we receive a follow-up survey from a company related to a product purchased or service provided. We may be presented with a satisfaction scale, as shown below.

### Satisfaction Scale

1------------2------------3------------4------------5

| Strongly disagree | Disagree | Undecided | Agree | Strongly agree |

The book-ends of the scale (easy way and best way) that I developed were put in place first. The real challenge was to stop and consider three other descriptors to place along the continuum. This is where unconstrained and creative thinking is needed. The figure below is an example of what I refer to as a leadership scale.

## Best Way Scale

```
1------------2------------3------------4------------5
```
| Easy | Safe | Fair | Right | Best |
| Way | Way | Way | Way | Way |

For me, and I hope for you, a leadership scale can simply be a way of looking at something, framing a situation, weighing options, choosing a position to take on a debated issue, or laying down the foundation of how you intend to lead.

In this scale, leaders can be reminded not to simply take the *easy way* out. That does not mean we should over-complicate matters, when decisiveness and keeping it simple are needed. *Best way* could get us thinking about *best practices*, which means that others have thought about the scenario you are facing or a closely related issue or topic before. From the experiences of others, you can discover a strongly recommended course of action to consider. Risk management teaches us as leaders to always consider safety, which is why *safe way* has a spot on the scale. Effective leaders take steps to prevent and mitigate risks, which vary considerably among industries.

Most leaders are in a *people* business. Somewhere along the line, we have all felt the impact of treatment that seemed unfair or inconsistent, so *fair way* is included in this scale. Not to be confused, by the way, with the fairway we hope to hit off the first tee. The concept of integrity influenced my thinking when introducing *right way* to the scale, as I was reminded about the often used four quadrant model designed to get leaders to consider how we do or don't do the right thing, the right way. The options are framed: 1) doing the wrong thing, the wrong way, 2) doing the wrong thing, the right way, 3) doing the right thing, the wrong way, and 4) doing the right thing, the right way.

You'll find leadership scales in each chapter, and provided collectively in the back of the book as a resource. I hope there is at least one that speaks to you. By all means, mark them up to reflect how you look at things, and make them your own. Even better, start developing your own leadership scales to represent your thought process around an issue that your team or company is facing. You may discover that you are better prepared to contribute a well thought out perspective that others may not have considered.

I discovered in my final decade of teaching, that presenting leadership scales as an activity enhanced both independent and reflective thinking. These scales enabled me to challenge others with at least an initial framework when considering a complex challenge. In training future leaders, I might simply say, "The wall to your left is yes, and the wall to your right is no". I would then share an ethical dilemma or a sticky situation a leader might encounter related to their field of interest, and invite them to take a stand by moving to one side of the room or the other. Generally, I only had one prepared question to pose once students were in place, "Why are you there"?

Typically, most students would move to one side or the other, but some would sit right in their seats. Just as we struggle at times to take a position on an important decision, those who stayed seated experienced this as well. As students shared why they were a "yes, no, or undecided", many thoughtful and thought-filled responses were shared. I might offer the opportunity for students to make a move if what they heard from a classmate across the room provided a position they now felt more inclined to support. Students who displayed independent thinking were most likely to re-frame the scenario or situation much differently than their peers.

Re-Framing (Chapter Seven) will provide some additional insight in reflective thinking as we are not done with the fatherly advice mentioned earlier. A second leadership scale (page 86) developed from the same quote will be presented there.

I had the great gift in the final decade of my career to be focused every day on preparing future leaders. The heartbeat of this book comes from the combination of career coaching, teaching, and leadership responsibilities I took on, and the lessons I learned. *Aspiring, developing, and emerging leaders* are the primary target audience I have kept in mind throughout this project. My hope is that the framework for this book, along with the stories and leadership principles and approaches included will also be of value to established leaders in many industries. Many of my stories and examples come from a career in sports and athletics, but I believe there are applicable lessons for anyone who discovers them here. Perhaps in reading, you will have powerful reminders of your stories, leadership lessons, triumphs, failures and how you bounced back from those.

Working on this book throughout the early years of retirement has resulted in a lot of thinking, sharing true stories that made me cry every time I reviewed them, and plenty of laughter, mostly at myself. "People are funny, and I am hilarious" is one of my favorite quips. It helps me to limit being judgmental of others and their actions, without first recognizing the abundance of weaknesses I exhibit daily. In recalling and sharing experiences from long ago, I am sure my memory is flawed. To those who find a story that involved you and my recollection is different than yours, please forgive me in advance. The content included is to the best of my recollection.

You may enjoy studying the Table of Contents and instinctively choosing a section or series of chapters to begin with. I tend to do just that when I start a new book on leadership, so I have kept that in mind as I developed this project. I like to write in leadership books I purchase, and have grown accustomed to noting in the Table of Contents, the order in which I plunged into each chapter and the date when that occurred. I believe you will find the sequence of sections (BELOW, BEHIND, ABOVE, and AHEAD) to be helpful and insightful if you follow from start to finish; however, decades of teaching reinforced for me just how different individuals are as learners. I may get just one chance with you, and the time is right now as you read this introduction. By all means, if you are adventurous and independent by nature, just select your first chapter—I'll meet you there.

# ↓ BELOW

A *firm foundation* is only as good as the mixture of concrete that formed it. That statement is sad but true in reports of entire housing developments with less than adequate standards adhered to for beautiful homes built upon footings now needing replacement.

Use these first three chapters to determine, confirm or re-examine deep-rooted principles that have—up to now—formed the foundation of your leadership. Perhaps you will discover some unplowed ground right beneath your feet, as you do some deep digging.

The example you set as a leader in your own character will set the tone for those you influence. Modeling integrity, establishing trust, and enhancing communication skills are the lead-off topics you are about to explore. Improving these leadership essentials will provide strong footing for every challenge you encounter.

# Chapter 1 - Integrity Switch

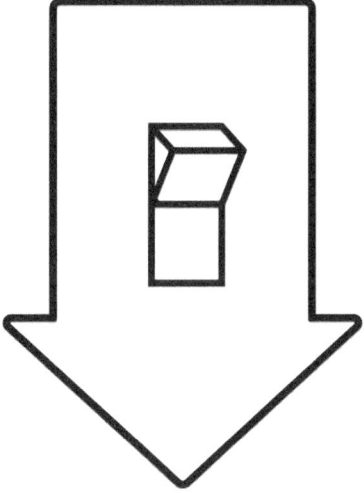

Imagine being a Jeopardy contestant when *Leadership Qualities* is revealed as a category. Surely you would buzz in quickly for, "What you do, how you act, or decisions you make when nobody is watching". Being careful of course to respond in the form of a question, "What is integrity?" would easily gain you control of the board.

If you jumped into this chapter without reading the preface, then you missed some important background on the title of this chapter and this book. For me, the idea of the switch coincides with our character "antennae" or "instincts". As a leadership quality, integrity will be among the top ten for any search you conduct, and often among the top three listed. Leadership books, articles published, and presentations delivered will typically carry this as a central theme.

Hopefully at a young age, honesty was part of our character development. Whether it was the feeling of a guilty conscience, or regret in telling a lie, most adults have a story about a lesson learned as a kid related to honesty, stealing or cheating. These experiences grow our character "antennae". Our leadership development needs that antennae to go off to avoid missteps and to stay in step with the standards we have developed for ourselves and those we lead. I propose with the integrity switch turned on, that leaders will sharpen their instincts and be quick not only to sense the antennae going off, but to respond to it.

You had the opportunity in the Introduction (page xxv) to discover the background and see an example of a tool I use called leadership scales. In framing the topic of integrity with a leadership scale, vehicle headlights came to mind. Headlights are a safety feature both for you and others you encounter. Safety features are designed to protect. If guarding your reputation is important to you, integrity is a must. Your integrity as a leader also protects your organization along with the partnerships and relationships attached to it. As I developed the scale below, *off* and *on* ended up embedded within and not on either end.

## Integrity Switch Scale

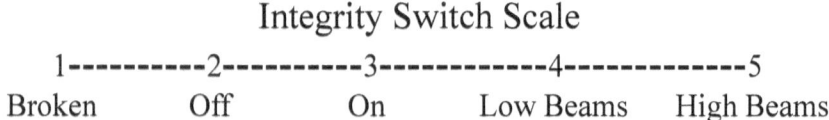

1-----------2-----------3-------------4--------------5
Broken        Off         On      Low Beams    High Beams

Automobile owners understandably assume their lights are always in working order. Now and then, a good Samaritan pulls up beside you at a stop light, gets your attention, and lets you know your right brake light is *broken*. You will need to pay to replace that light, but damage to a professional reputation caused by a lack of integrity can be much more costly.

While turning your headlights *on* after dark is a necessity, we occasionally get a friendly signal from an oncoming car, and only then realize that our lights are *off.* Sometimes, we need help from others to see some things we don't see. That can be true with integrity as well. We need trusted advisors at times, to help us maintain our integrity when ethical dilemmas emerge.

## LEADERSHIP needs to be a team sport!

I really believe that. Surround yourself with others you can rely on in stressful moments. Those are the ones who know you well enough to say, "Well, here is what I think you will do."

What about those especially dark moments that leaders experience? We do find ourselves alone and in a tough spot from time to time. This is when we need the strength of our convictions to guide us. *High beams* are needed when deep fog limits our visibility on the road. Days arrive for all of us as leaders when controversy, conflict or a crisis demands our full attention. Those will be the times where you will need your integrity switch on full tilt.

So, what makes leadership rewarding? You get to make a difference. You will be part of celebration and breakthrough days—where hard work pays off. You will also gain great satisfaction as you watch your investment in others pay off, through their growth and development. Learn how to step back, and push others forward. Maybe those are the moments for *low beams*, just enough light to assure others you are there.

In the chapter review section, you will have a chance to outline this scale, and personalize it in a way that will benefit you. Let's explore more foundational concepts that can assure you of rock-solid footing, for the leadership trail that you are pursuing.

# Foundational Qualities

Mission statements typically reflect core values that will be expected to be modeled by everyone in the community. They sure look good on paper, and the process of drafting and finalizing a mission statement can unify a leadership team. A mission statement is foundational to the work, and how that work will be assessed. In the business world, leaders look at quarterly reports to gauge the most recent results, compare those to previous quarters, and perhaps re-assess upcoming quarterly projections. Are the foundational qualities represented by our mission statement part of that quarterly report, or is the profit/loss or ROI the central focus?

Our competitive season in the world of sports is evaluated both internally and externally. What about our impact in the off-season or all the work that goes into planning and preparing for the next pre-season? Let's stay with the coach as a leader, and see what can be applied in other leadership roles. What are the non-negotiables in your written team expectations? What does it take for someone to get a spot, and keep a spot on your roster? The foundational qualities you value will emerge as you answer those questions. In addition to integrity, any number of personal character attributes will be considered: loyalty, honesty, and a team-first mindset might be chief among those. One of the difficult, yet rewarding aspects of growing as a leader is the necessity to self-assess continuously. Will you be intentional in that challenge?

At your core, what do you believe? At your core, what do you believe in? Your responses to those two questions should be central for what you will stand for as a leader. Start there in identifying the foundational qualities that you intend to be evident to all of those who interact with your team.

Now, I'd like to push back if all of this, on the surface, seems too elementary. Most coaches reading this are part of a larger organization.

Their program is but one of many, and that program is led by a director of all teams. That director has foundational qualities that are part of a larger mission statement. To what degree does the coach in the earlier discussion need to ensure that their leadership, their mission statement aligns? To what degree can there be unique aspects for an individual team amidst a backdrop of many teams? When asked in an interview for a head coaching job, if you have any questions, start with that one.

So, let's bring some application to leadership in general by considering those who are the bottom line: the business owner, the corporate or non-profit Board of Directors, CEOs, or commissioners as just a few examples. The challenge in all cases is to determine the foundational qualities that have been identified, and then ensure that every aspect of branding, marketing, and promoting the work of that organization is marked by those qualities.

"Don't forget", as one business leader shared with me, "You are your most important investment, and leadership development starts with you. You must focus on a growth mindset. Invest in yourself. Put time into growing the quality of your leadership skills".

In addition, your actions (the way you lead) will be observed in how you evaluate and reward those who exemplify those foundational qualities. How you consistently identify and address words and actions that do not align with what your company stands for, will also be noticed. The values you are looking for will need to be modeled daily. Our imperfections as people will creep into our words and actions as leaders—when they do—we must identify those moments and correct ourselves.

## Un-mistake-able Qualities

I have grown accustomed with great enthusiasm to facilitating a rather simple activity for those who have sought me out as a mentor. Let me offer it to you—starting with two simple questions. The next time you apply for a new job, or seek to advance in the company you are with— who will you undoubtedly seek out to provide a recommendation letter?

If you asked them to include three un-mistake-able qualities about you, what would make that list?

As you pause to consider that—please push back against the notion that you are being boastful. Yes, there can be some pride vs. humility tension in this activity. So, don't start with your opinion about yourself—just jot down what you have earned in the eyes of someone else. Keep in mind, your supporter has their own *integrity* on the line on your behalf, when they submit letters of support. I can only speak for myself, because I write plenty of those letters. I must choose my words carefully, because they must be accurate. My favorite letters are those where I feel no restraint, and share something like, "In no time at all, you will see these un-mistake-able qualities in this candidate. . ."

My purpose in directing this activity links to a later chapter (page 105) where confidence will be discussed. Something I believe about leaders and leadership is that you must know and appreciate yourself. Doubting yourself as a leader need not be a constant companion. Whether someone is watching or not, your self-confidence is strengthened when you know the qualities you will bring day after day. Identifying strengths you can count on daily from yourself will be a form of self-encouragement and self-assurance. Recognizing your weaknesses is equally important. You will need both of these. Disclaimer—just being transparent here. If humility and gratitude aren't part of your leadership foundation, then what am I attempting to offer in this book, will likely be unhelpful.

When you are ready to make your own list, am I hopeful that *integrity* makes your top three? Actually, I hope that without reading this—you can count on *integrity*. You have been asked or you will be asked in an interview to outline your strengths. Be prepared. Identify those for yourself and be ready to share them.

Chapter Four (page 41) will reinforce the need to identify our weaknesses and those areas that need to improve or be changed. Chapter Six (page 63) will pivot to the importance of focusing and enhancing our strengths. Keep this activity in mind when you get there, and start exploring those topics. Take the *integrity switch* challenge. Define it for yourself. Turn it on, and keep it on.

## Chapter One Review

- Flip on your integrity switch and keep it blazing.
- Leadership needs to be a team sport.
- Identify the un-mistake-able qualities you can count on daily from yourself.

1 - List your core values below. What are your foundational qualities?

2 - Now, name three un-mistake-able qualities about yourself. Don't be humble. Pull out the last cover letter you wrote and include them below.

1.

2.

3.

3 – What expectations have you made (or will you make) crystal clear to your team members? What does it take to make your team, to prosper on your team, and to remain on your team?

4 – Your turn – how will you arrange your Integrity Switch leadership scale (see page 2)?

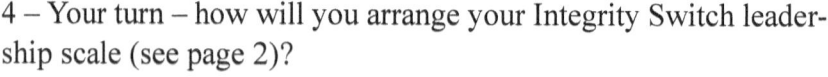

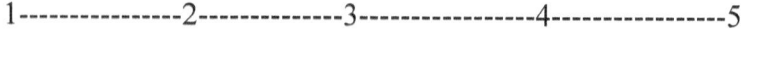

Options could include: broken   dim   hazards   high beams low beams   on   off

5 – Consider the following pressing questions for leaders that relate to this chapter:

What defines you?

What do you believe?

What do you believe in?

Who do you work for?

Who actually benefits from your work?

# Chapter 2 – The "Trust" Process

"Trust the process". That is an *interesting* response from a leader to stakeholders with reasonable and probing questions related to the launch of some new initiative. Implied is the notion that "You'll see" at the conclusion of this undertaking that this trust was well-placed. Rather than providing straightforward explanations, the spokesperson seems to be imploring those seeking answers to simply have faith. But, faith in what? Shouldn't the trust be *in those leading* instead of *on the process*?

I'll offer an amended version, "Trust a *trustworthy* process". What might that look like? *The trust process* is greatly enhanced when progress is reported regularly, and even better, feedback is solicited. Looking back as a follower, I always appreciated simple announcements from a leader describing an upcoming change. I found it helpful to know the steps that were planned, along with when and how the change would be implemented. I appreciated even more, when opportunities to participate were offered.

Whether you are a veteran leader or just now getting opportunities to lead a process—what impression will you make? Beyond trusting you, will others declare at the conclusion of their involvement, that the experience was inspiring to be part of? Exceptional leaders have that kind of impact. As you enact change or develop a new idea, developing trust is on the line for those following your leadership. Examine the trust scale that follows and reflect on past experiences that may have included these descriptors.

## The Trust Scale

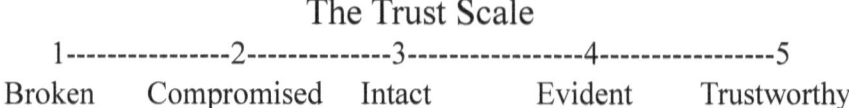

1----------------2--------------3-----------------4-----------------5
Broken      Compromised    Intact        Evident      Trustworthy

Building trust *is* a process. The last thing we want to see when we initiate action is for trust among relationships to be *broken*. Poorly handled discussions or conversations are often identified as the culprit for causing the damage. Leading a significant process of change without developing a communication plan is unwise. When communication breaks down or is absent, trust can be *compromised* in working relationships.

Despite a genuine desire to enhance the experience of those we lead, there will be times when we're not successful in that regard. Developing the habit of self-reflection can help. Most leaders will admit or at least discover that they over-reached in pursuing and planning a change. A careful and critical review might reveal that the resources needed were under-estimated, or that a more experienced team member should have been at the helm. Despite our good intentions, the faith of our followers can be *compromised.*

These scenarios represent growth opportunities for us as leaders. We don't need to throw in the towel, and avoid the next process of change or progress. You can keep trust *intact* by going back to your followers and listening to their perspectives. Ask how a recently completed process could have, perhaps should have, been better. A debrief that is candid, and includes dissenting views, can help trust develop. Display integrity consistently with your words and actions when tackling challenges. The team you are developing will take notice. As they follow suit, a culture where mutual trust is clearly *evident,* can develop.

Since trust is a two-way street, another perspective needs to be discussed. Leaders do need to pay attention when one or more individuals regularly challenge your leadership. Individual objections and opposing views can be healthy, but not when it turns into some form of obstruction. There are times for frank discussion with team members to determine their level of support. In those conversations, reinforce the values that support the mission of your team, organization, or company. Hopefully, that reminder will allow you to move ahead without further attention on their participation or employment status.

Can I trust you? In life and in leadership, that question comes our way, and at times we are asking that question. When, "Yes" is lived out in that response and proven over time to be the case, integrity will have been on display. We become *trustworthy* in large part, by how we lead and handle ourselves with others. Hopefully those observable actions will bring you to the place where you won't need to say, "Trust the process".

Just an aside to coaches about process before we proceed to our next topic. The trust process is presented above clearly related to leadership, not in the context of athlete's performing. Focusing on the process (performance) over product (results) in competitive situations is a much different discussion. Our competitive teams trained and competed with specific performance objectives in mind. One of the goals was to keep our performers in the moment, and ready for the next touch of the ball, and not on the scoreboard.

## Credibility - Lead by Example

"Leading by example" usually finds its' way into the first sixty seconds of any leadership presentation, and rightfully so. What are the characteristics of your leadership where the example you set merits following? The answer to that will eventually be established by the high character behaviors that you model. A mindset of valuing each day while putting your best foot forward, might be the key to developing credibility.

There is no *secret to success*, but there are professional habits that will contribute to a successful career. Simply showing up every day and putting in an honest day's work is a great place to start. Repeating this approach daily surely enhances the chances of being successful, and provides a great model for others to follow.

Need a suggestion on how to show others that they can trust and count on you? Start with attitude and effort. Legendary UCLA men's basketball coach, John Wooden, developed a wonderful tool for team builders called the Pyramid of Success. Take a close inspection and you will notice that enthusiasm (an attitude) and industriousness (a descriptor of effort) are two of the five characteristics at the base of the pyramid. In fact, these are the two cornerstones. I suspect he placed them there as essential to a strong foundation.[4]

> A positive attitude and consistent effort and energy are foundational in developing credibility.

People are always watching, and they will notice who arrives early to be on time, and who is willing to stay to get a job done, or take on an unexpected challenge. Bringing a positive attitude to a task at hand, especially when some type of above and beyond effort is needed, will pay great dividends. Leading enthusiastically when fulfilling a commitment sets a great example, and may even be contagious for those in your team environment. Remember, however, that how we handle commitments in the work/life balancing act will also set an example for others.

One of the ways to set appropriate boundaries with time demands, is to place trust in others. Delegate responsibilities to those under your wing to create some space in your own schedule. Test yourself in this process. Can you give them some space, and provide guidance when they request it? Or, are you a bit of a micro-manager? Try to remember how your leadership blossomed when confidence was shown in you.

Challenges with time management emerge quickly, especially as you take on more leadership duties. Leaders must determine how to fulfill commitments both on the job, and at home. Even as you make those determinations, you will feel the tension in making choices daily.

So, choose wisely, and save some enthusiasm and energy for life outside of the office.

Additionally, leaders discover that advance planning designed to assist in completing tasks, will compete with the dreaded habit of procrastination. Do all you can to avoid earning that label. Be certain that your followers observe strong organizational skills in you. Effective leaders will need to confront team members who give themselves permission to miss deadlines and become comfortable offering excuses. Be sure that those flaws are not observable in you.

Credibility will be challenged by the expectations that leaders put in place. Our athletics program required each coach to provide student-athletes with written behavioral expectations. Inevitably, our players did not meet one of the expectations. I needed wisdom in dealing with each situation individually, but with as much consistency as possible. Handling situations will test our credibility, but also allows for creative problem solving.

Here is a slightly different take on this topic. In leadership roles, do you take the time to catch others doing something right? This is a tactic well worth polishing, as many parents have discovered. To pursue this strategy, you need to be close enough to the action to catch someone. I think of USA Women's Soccer Coach, Tony DiCicco, related to this topic. He was one of the authors of a book with the title, *Catch Them Being Good: Everything you need to know to successfully coach girls.* [5]

In order to accomplish this, we might need to get out from behind the desk to catch those we are leading doing good things. Management by walking around (MBWA) is often noted as an important strategy to include in your approach to leading. I enjoy watching episodes of *Undercover Boss*. In this reality TV series, executives decide to discover what is *really* happening within their companies by disguising themselves and infiltrating the ranks. Unsuspecting employees share unfiltered input on the company, along with personal obstacles with the boss.

Eventually, the workers experience the CEO *reveal*, often with heart-warming scenes where significant personal needs get some assistance. In some cases, highly effective and dedicated personnel have at times, received promotions to a leadership level to help solve problems illustrated during the episode. Very often, these individuals have labored faithfully and effectively for years. Seemingly out of nowhere, they are *caught* in the act and rewarded for their dedication. Do you have a favorite MBWA story? If not, then take the challenge, and see what insight you can gain just by walking around your people.

Let me share mine—which occurred in my formative years as an athletic administrator. A club sport with a strong roster, an experienced coach, and a solid schedule was gaining popularity on campus. Highly engaged student leaders had been campaigning annually for their sport to become part of our intercollegiate program. As the academic year started; my direct supervisor informed me that I was tasked with preparing a formal report and recommendation. The charge was simple. Should this club sport be elevated to varsity status? The report was due at the conclusion of the spring semester.

I realized early on that my biggest struggle centered on *how to take a position* that I could support on this important decision. During the Fall semester, I worked with the club leaders to obtain a few varsity level games for their upcoming season—so the schedule was on my desk for some time. I began to study that emerging schedule—which sparked an idea. I circled a date and time on my calendar that would allow for a direct observation that I believed would show me the position I should take. Not one soul knew about that day and time, nor the significance I was placing on it.

When that day arrived, I left my office and walked to the appointed observation site. This particular Friday afternoon (early May as I recall) was very sunny. Our waterfront campus was sparkling. Arriving fifteen minutes prior to the next scheduled practice of that team. . . . I was able to see a steady stream of students headed off campus to start their weekend. Some would surely get to the nearby beaches. The same choices were available to all the students participating in this club sport. I was positioned on the corner of the team's practice field. The coach was already in the center of the field when I arrived. Cones had been set up, and well before 4:00, the entire roster had gathered on the sideline.

The team had been soundly defeated the day before by the strongest varsity team on their schedule. That had not been difficult to anticipate when I noted that match-up—months earlier. The response to that competition was what I was after. Precisely at the scheduled 4:00 practice time, the coach blew the whistle and gathered the group. After a brief review of the competition the previous day, and a few comments on the next opponent, the team began a well-rehearsed warm-up. I stayed long enough to see some spirited effort during a few drills, and some good signs of comradery during drink breaks.

I returned to my office and wrote a very brief memo to my supervisor with my final recommendation. I was able to take a supportive position, and as I recall the message was, "The team is operating on par with our current intercollegiate programs. The transition next season as a varsity program will be quite smooth." Years later, when I first heard about MBWA, that experience came to mind.

To build credibility, lead by example with effort that can be counted on, and enthusiasm that moves others to join in. Care enough about those you lead to get behind the scenes and observe them in the tough or non-glamorous parts of the job. Let's move now to one last topic that is often mentioned when establishing trust within any type of team.

## Transparency / Confidentiality

I think we have established that leaders need to be trusted. Whether making changes or moving an organization forward, leaders are putting trust on the line. One of the most significant leadership considerations connected to trust is transparency. Calls for transparency are commonplace once any type of team or company is informed of new ventures or impending changes. Leaders could anticipate that by providing background information and draft proposals with initial options under consideration. Of course, that will generate questions, and your responses are likely to be unsatisfactory for some. In no time at all, "The need for full transparency" becomes the discussion, and not the advancement opportunity being proposed.

I often hear author and business leader, Max DePree, referenced in relation to the adage that the first responsibility of a leader is to define reality.[6] Here is a reality about transparency—full transparency works in a perfect world. The problem is we don't live or lead in a perfect world. We will be naïve as leaders, if we don't recognize that there are many realistic obstacles to full transparency. Let's look at a few, and consider the impact on trust.

Confidentiality might be front-and-center as a barrier for full transparency. Legal and ethical considerations come to mind that can and should prohibit sharing of information. Leaders discover early on that at times, healthy discussions will have information shared that needs to be kept confidential. We need to pro-actively address this. Wisdom is needed, and all leaders likely develop this over time, when someone comes to you in confidence. Aspects of an individual's formal evaluation, compensation and contractual details for an employee, especially in a private organization may be entitled to confidentiality. You can avoid damage to relationships, and to your organization by ensuring all stakeholders recognize the need for information at times to be kept confidential.

I've never heard a better definition of culture, than the simple phrase, "How we do things here". Communicate decisively when a question can't be answered because of confidentiality. Leaders need to protect their culture from time to time, by guarding sensitive information. We also must recognize the vulnerability that some may have in approaching a leader for a difficult discussion. When someone approaches you with hesitation, consider pausing to ask questions that will help you understand sources of that caution. This delay will allow the conversation to begin by defining the extent to which any information shared can be held in confidence. This should help bring some comfort to both parties, and clear the way for an open dialogue.

A culture of trust probably develops one conversation at a time, however, leaders have limits on availability and access. Daily schedules get filled quickly. In spite of that, leaders often make a point to declare they have an "open door" policy. A word of caution should that approach describe you. Do you have a schedule with openings? Transparency is much more observable during face-to-face conversations. What happens when a team member sees your door open, but you can't give that time to them? You potentially can lose a little credibility.

Perhaps defining your open-door policy will help. Just take it a step further by communicating how they can count on you to follow up when you have a line outside your door. Responding to the post-it notes you find or follow-up emails from someone who has been struggling to find your door open is critical. When possible, re-tracing their steps and appearing in their doorway to connect is sure to get their attention. Showing up shows you care, and it will be appreciated.

Companies, businesses and teams are comprised of individuals selected for an area of expertise and strength. How can we maximize the experience and abilities available to us? When difficult or complex challenges or issues arise, put those talents to the test. Keep a watchful eye out for those who are adding value to your organization, and be sure you are transparent as you include them in any problem-solving process. This gives you a chance to confirm positive qualities you have been observing in them. Be clear in describing the role each team member is being assigned, and make sure they know they can check in with you as needed.

We won't get every process we lead out on right. We will be disappointed at times not only with the results, but ourselves. We may be brave enough to even say that out loud to those we are leading. Our integrity switch helps us do more of that. The next process we lead can be better as long as we first interrogate any past missteps openly. Credibility as a leader can gain traction not just from successful endeavors, but also from the character exhibited in setbacks.

Keep this in mind—trust takes time to develop in relationships. Our credibility can be damaged in just a few, short moments. You will have plenty of moments of truth that will test you, and shape your leadership. I have always been impressed with thoughtful, genuine, and authentic people. Seek to bring those characteristics to your work as a leader. Transparency and trust will flow out of that intentionality.

By the way, we hear experienced leaders mention, "trust your gut", or "trust your antennae". How is that developed? Integrity, trust, and other foundational qualities you establish and exercise daily will guide your moral compass. Be the leader, you intend to be.

## Chapter Two Review

- Trust a trustworthy process.
- There is no secret to success, rather show up and put in an honest day's work, then repeat daily.
- Leading by example means that example must be observed in some way.
- A positive attitude and consistent effort and energy are foundational in developing credibility

1 - Reflect on the phrase "trust the process". What factors do you value on the topic of building trust?

2 - What makes your list of essentials for building and maintaining credibility?

3 - Define: Leading by example

4 - What will be the key observations of your followers, that will enable them to describe you as transparent?

5 – Identify and describe one non-negotiable for the culture you are leading, or intend to lead in the future. (What must every follower of your leadership need to know in no uncertain terms?)

6 – What is your favorite MBWA story, or some lesson learned from getting out from behind the desk.

# Chapter 3 - Three C's:
# Communication, Conversations,
# Conflict

G race. What does Eric Enstrom have to do with the idea of saying grace? Does a picture come to mind that clearly depicts the act of saying grace? How about Eric's photo? In 1918, he snapped a photo of an elderly man, sitting at a table with his forehead leaning into clenched hands. I bet you can visualize this image. Apparently in 2002, Minnesota designated this as the state photograph.

The bearded man with silver hair is sitting in front of a loaf of bread, a bowl of soup, and what appears to be a big, thick Bible with folded eyeglasses sitting on top of it. Charles Wilden is the man in the photo and it was taken in Bovey, Minnesota. He appears to be praying silently, and I suspect that gratitude is being expressed as part of this inner dialogue.

When you google *essential communication skills for leaders*, you will notice that this book is not on the first page of that search. Many leadership gurus have filled that space with very helpful and thoughtful suggestions. Here is my approach. I have framed this chapter with three words that need to be linked, as we interact with others in developing, building, and maintaining relationships in our sphere of influence. As we look at communication, conversations, and conflict, consider the following questions:

- Why does introspection about inner dialogue and self-talk matter?
- What aspects of communication should we consider in tandem fashion?
- Is it true that "the conversation is the relationship"?
- What conversational skills can be helpful when confronting conflict?

At least once a week, my wife will ask me, "What did you say?" to which my response is, "Oh nothing, I was just mumbling to myself". We talk to ourselves all day long. At times we find ourselves daydreaming, preoccupied or rehearsing for an upcoming interaction, or even more often replaying a recent conversation. "A penny for your thoughts?", is a question that at times pulls us back into the present by someone who can tell we are caught up in some deep thought.

Coaches can be a great help to athletes who may not stop to examine their personal patterns of self-talk. The team is down one with two seconds to go. A back-up point guard is on the free throw line with two chances to put her team in the lead. What does she hear from that voice in the back of her head? Look at the phrases in the ladder of success below.

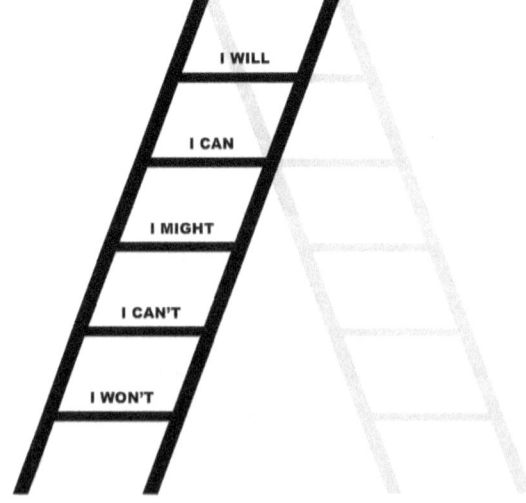

She takes a few dribbles, and looks at the rim. Are negative thoughts down near the bottom of the ladder drowning out the shouts of confidence that sit atop of it? We can all relate to these phrases that have stopped, stalled, or motivated us, because growth means overcoming obstacles.

Moving up the ladder from *I won't* to *I will* when applied to challenges we face are pretty good examples of what we say to ourselves. I've seen depictions of ladders like this one with as many as eleven rungs. I selected five phrases just to get you started. You will be asked in the chapter review to develop your own. We will come back to this concept more fully in Chapter Ten (page 132).

Before we take on the task as leaders to manage others, I sure hope we have taken the time to grow in the area of managing ourselves. Have you established a standard for yourself that requires your actions to align with your words? What do you intend to do when they don't? Will your trusty antennae go off when you start to veer from the values and principles you hold dear?

So, I value *gratitude, loyalty, authenticity and humility*. How do I remind myself daily about those things? Am I like Charles in the photo, taking a moment to recognize what I do have to be *grateful* for and expressing that in an intimate, meaningful, and soulful way? How often do you stop for quiet moments of introspection?

What causes me to be convicted and committed to displaying *loyalty* when I am confronted by something that could cause me to stray from that? "Team-first", is such a great motto for a team, and relates directly to *loyalty*. Taking the time to consider our words and actions are all examples of inner dialogue.

## All leaders made mistakes.

When you almost instantly regret something you have said, being *authentic* may require that you respond right away. Correcting ourselves or clarifying something we have said or stated is emblematic of *humility* and may arise from the time taken for some self-examination. As leaders, we will expect our followers to be open to objections, and corrections that we point out. Modeling self-correction will help.

One step you might consider, if you feel like your inner dialogue and self-talk needs some work is to begin journaling. Dare I suggest you take this on as a new habit with a hand-held journal and a pen? Much of this book originated from journal entries. Often, I never knew what was on my mind, until I read it back once the ink was dry.

I hope that *integrity switch* starts to slip into your lexicon as you determine how you intend to handle a sticky situation. Pay attention to that inner voice and your leadership instincts. Some time ago, I happened to be in a social setting where I observed a young professional who I have known a long time, who was wrestling with an ethical dilemma. This leader's antennae was going off related to a decision that needed to be made. The leader was asked if advice had been sought and received from others more experienced in this type of business scenario. The leader responded affirmatively, but decided against following the advice. Why?

Because that would mean employing lower standards than those he had established. Kudos to you leaders, when you follow this example.

## Communication & Conversation Tandems

I have had a passion for coaching education for decades. I was blessed to go through some great training with a few organizations that equipped me to help other coaches. One of the first resources in that professional development journey that I bumped into was an early edition of *Coaching Successfully*. The author, Rainer Martens, outlined three dimensions of communication that I almost always refer to when some aspect of a workshop relates to communication. Martens established a nice framework for others to consider around, what I would call, communication tandems. These tandems consist of two words linked and in relationship with each other, that we would do well to work on. Each of the words can stand alone and be defined separately, but can also work in conjunction with each other.[7]

*Content and emotion* comprise our first duo, and well worth reflecting on as we think about our communication style. There are times, when the content of our message, or directions for an assignment are very straightforward. Little or no emotion is in play, nor is it needed. At other times, it may be that what is needed is a little emotion to get our point across.

I know some of my former players like to talk about some memorable time-outs they experienced with me. There were moments on the sidelines, frankly, where the one clear observation was that my players were distracted. I think at times their minds were somewhere else, or there was a lack of cohesion happening within the team ranks, and that had them out of focus. A time-out in those situations probably featured a little emotion, if for no other reason than to get their attention. The content of what I would be saying might not be negative at all, but the delivery observed by those sitting in the stands may have appeared that way.

Martens also highlighted *verbal and nonverbal*. As leaders gain experience interviewing applicants for an open staff position, we begin to pay attention to nonverbal cues. Young professionals use mock interviews to prepare for these all-important meetings. Public speaking and other leadership opportunities sharpen our use of nonverbal skills. Gestures, smiles, and the occasional thumb up are all examples of ways we can use nonverbal cues to get a message across.

*Silence* also resides in our nonverbal category. Teachers learn to allow for silence. If we ask an effective question, the silence could simply mean the listeners are engaged in thinking it over. Likewise, we receive deep and probing questions, that seem to stop us in our tracks. There is nothing wrong with replying, "That is a great question. I need time to think that through."

Silence at times can do the heavy lifting, especially when strong emotions are in play. No words will alter the feelings of someone with a heavy heart. Providing our quiet presence, even for a few short moments, certainly lets them know you care. Finally, there are also times when choosing silence may be the wise path. Communication comes to us in many forms beyond direct conversation, including emails, texts, and voice messages. Leaders need to determine, establish, and delineate when those are and are not the appropriate means of communication. Basic administrative and organizational questions and responses can be highly effective using those forms. Be alert however, for messages and messengers using non-direct methods of conversation on topics or issues that clearly should be handled face to face.

All leaders would do well to carefully consider the balance between *sending and receiving*, another tandem shared by Martens. What would we expect from a dictatorial leader? Lots of orders. Obviously, we want to be clear when providing direction, but we also need to know that we are understood. As teachers, we are trained to check for understanding, and this is a good rule of thumb as well for us as leaders. When I think about receiving in the realm of communication, it means I need to take listening seriously.

Active listening is one of the best approaches to improving our receiving skills. Finding a few simple words or phrases to simply acknowledge what was shared is a solid approach. Playing back what you just heard, or injecting a follow-up question shows that you are in the discussion with them. Active listening does not mean you should finish the sentences of the person speaking to you. Proceed with caution as well with feeling the need to always relate to someone's situation by sharing a similar one of our own. That approach may provide helpful insight to that person, but often people just want to be heard.

A second resource I have found helpful is Susan Scott's *Fierce Conversations: Achieving Success at work and in life one conversation at a time*. Essentially, the author recounts a number of situations as a consultant to CEO's and other business leaders, where she was brought in to look behind the scenes to uncover underlying issues that needed to be addressed. The front cover of the 1st edition offers a definition of fierce as *robust, intense, strong, powerful, passionate, eager, and unbridled.*[8] I have selected the five descriptors below to depict a wide range of approaches to conversing.

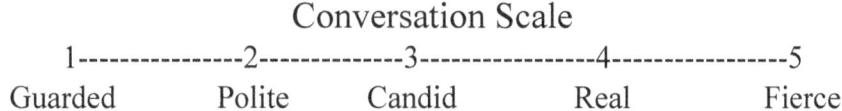

You can have some fun marking this scale up for your use. There will be no shortage of additional terms you can swap out for those above, including: honest, pointed, deep, persuasive, intense, passive, aggressive, and passive-aggressive.

One phrase from Scott that jumped off the page for me was "The conversation is the relationship". How is your company, organization or team a "people business"? Do you think of it that way? If you employ, deploy, supervise, direct, organize, lead, or team up with other people, then relationships with others will demand your attention. Building, maintaining, and sustaining relationships needs to be part of the foundational work that we do as leaders.

Over the years, as I spent a good deal of time preparing and planning material either for the classroom or upcoming events, I paired up a few words of my own that you may find useful. Consider how linking these essential elements together could enhance relationships.

***Hearing and Listening***. It may not show for those who know me best, but I have been working on my listening skills with great determination for many years. Thankfully those who know me best, seem to be some of the most gracious people I know. They recognize what I have known a long time, that I am a work in progress . . .let me pause here. . . I sure hope in that pause, your inner dialogue clicked in and you said to yourself, "So am I".

A veteran colleague of mine, Coach Naomi Graves, has said more than once, and always emphatically, "Listening is the number one leadership skill". I listened to you, but did I hear you? I heard you, but did I listen to you? As you consider those two questions, also factor in whether you tend to be a slow processor or fast processor. I tend to be a fast processor. I constantly need to remind myself that others could be just the opposite. I wonder at times, if my processing pace is by nature or nurture.

I coached well over 1,000 college volleyball matches. Our sport places twelve players in two separated but congested playing areas. Rallies feature rapid and intermittent touches that range from a ball landing on the top of an outstretched hand on the floor to a spike contacted near or well above the height of a basketball rim. Opposing defenders of that pounded attack could be within ten feet, requiring lightning-like reaction times. Rallies can go on for sixty seconds. That is a lot of action to process. That was my work environment. I would think that contributed to a mind that races all the time.

How has your work environment impacted your communication? Are there sounds and noises that make hearing difficult? Is your work space (whether remote or in a more traditional setting) set up where distractions often detract from listening carefully? Go discover that, mull it over, and take one step to improve it. I will give you one example.

The last version of my faculty office was pretty standard. I liked having my desk situated so I faced the door, and could easily greet those popping in or walking by. I had two chairs for guests on either side of the office door. On most days, my desk clearly exhibited a very ingrained multi-task style. Everything on my desk presented distractions for me, and those distractions were not going to help my listening skills. During one-on-one academic advising and at other times, when I had meetings in my office, I often made one simple adjustment. I would move to one of the two chairs away from my desk, and sit facing my guest. What can you change to enhance your listening skills? Be fully present. Work on making eye contact, and eliminate potential distractions.

***Informing and Sharing.*** Most leadership books will include a number of leadership theories. Often, among the topics presented will be the contrast of two styles of leadership: transactional and transformational. Transactional is generally discussed in relation to tasks, and could describe a leader focused on the present. A transformational leader may be regarded as more of a visionary, and a motivator with relationships as a priority.

Clearly at times, our communication as a leader is simply informative. A quick memo or email to all staff that the annual company picnic has a date change, might be a good example of completing a transaction. Following up a year-end review of an employee with several comment boxes full of suggestions of how to move from *meets expectations* to *exceeds expectations* might be more of a transformational type of exchange.

Where can this brief focus on these two words help you immediately? Think about mentoring opportunities you have in supervisory duties. We *inform* frequently as a supervisor, and that may take the form of instructing, directing, and training. Opportunities will also emerge to do some mentoring. We can *share* from our experiences, to guide and encourage, especially when we are asked for insight.

**Intended and Interpreted.** We are about to transition to the topic of conflict, so I saved this final pairing for last. Leaders will have sticky situations. Sadly, some of those will be of our own making when a message you *intended* to convey is not well received. Even when we take time to form messages, we must realize that as soon as they are delivered, we lose some control. We don't get to determine how those on the receiving end will *interpret* that message. You've probably been on both sides of this. Conversations move quickly. We might feel offended right on the spot by a comment, or we may have a delayed reaction. Those conversing with us can have the same experience.

If "The conversation is the relationship", then a willingness to work through difficult exchanges is an attitude we need to work on. Asking for clarification offers someone a chance to do just that. Offering to clarify when that is requested, is the best you can do at that moment. Most people are pretty forgiving. I believe that the idea of "working through" things together is essential for the health of any relationship.

As we are gaining experience as leaders, we will have some

healthy and normal fears around difficult conversations. How can we be assertive and straightforward, yet gracefully direct? These are the scenarios where you have time to consider how the messages you *intend* to send will be *interpreted*. You may find yourself wrestling with or avoiding a conversation, because deep down, you are concerned that it could hurt the relationship. Keep in mind, that the simple act of intentionally requesting a chance to meet, shows that you care enough to talk things over.

Almost every aspect of leadership is impacted in some way by communication. Your communication style will garner opinions from others who interact with you. Those impressions will result in the degree to which you are seen as assertive, direct, open, or transparent, just to name a few. As a leader, you likely have developed by now a communication style that feels natural and comfortable for you. High performing teams have leaders who reportedly average nearly six positive comments for every negative one. Perhaps that should inform how we engage in conversations as the team leader!

## Confronting Conflict

Buckle your seatbelt because conflict, our next "C" is coming your way. Every leader will be involved somewhat routinely in some aspect of conflict. We create our own. Keep that in mind. Decision-making will be explored in Chapter Ten (page 124), but is appropriate to mention here. Leaders make dozens of decisions every day. We make decisions, procrastinate on decisions, and regret some decisions.

Decisions impact others,
and some of that impact will cause conflict.

Leaders do need to become aware of other sources of conflict, but there is some wisdom in considering first how our own words, actions and inactions affect others. Hopefully, communication and conversation fundamentals presented earlier will help you to improve in this area.

*Relational conflicts* will occur in a people business. Friction between co-workers is not uncommon in any industry. Internal rivalries are waged at times within a team or work force that creates a drag on the momentum you are trying to build. Identifying ill effects of internal rivalries is needed.

Some of the athletes I coached that I admired the most were those who were essentially battling each other daily for a spot in the line-up. However, once the match had begun, some of these internal competitors set great examples for their peers by how genuinely supportive they were for the one who got the nod to play instead of them. That attitude takes a good deal of emotional IQ. The hope as a coach was that the teammates would recognize that my playing time decisions did not need to hurt the relationships among them. More often than not, team members in those circumstances tend to shy away and distance themselves from each other.

Apply some of these concepts in building your team and assessing internal strains. Department heads reporting to you are competing for budget requests, personnel additions, and your attention. The dreaded *toxic atmosphere* may start with internal rivalries, and first show up in side conversations about someone not present. Leaders must be pro-active in reminding team members of the essential elements of unified teams. We must also describe openly, the common pitfalls that can crush team unity.

Team building initiatives will be needed for you to lead high performing teams. Leaders need to ensure that their, "Why we are here" messages are crystal clear, and reinforced. Expressing appreciation, acknowledging success, and rewarding outstanding teamwork are some good strategies to build *feelings of pride, fellowship, and common loyalty.* Those feelings are the definition of *espirit de corps.* I always loved when that phrase was mentioned around the idea of synergy and positive vibes that have been developed within some sort of team.

Conflict will also arise around tasks, duties, and responsibilities especially when some of those things need to change with individuals or a sub group. Some extremes that might be helpful to this topic would include each of the following.

1. Downsizing. That is a frightening word in many work spaces. I am confident there are many available resources you can find that will outline the common mistakes associated with this. Keeping the three C's in mind, what message do you intend to be received when you announce that downsizing is under consideration? When you go home that night, imagine how many dining room table discussions are centered on this messaging. Your people may take it as a warning, or perhaps a promise. Either way, if you stand in their shoes, I am sure you will determine effective ways to be truthful, but as encouraging as possible.

2. "We are moving in a new direction". How many ESPN moments capture that most common phrase as the Director of Athletics or General Manager explains why the coach has been fired? Hearing of a new direction always makes me wonder about the mission of that organization. Has the mission changed direction? How about the core values, are we changing direction and renaming them now? I admit that I do wonder if consideration is ever given to simply expressing, "In assessing our coach, we have determined that the expectations we had, have not been met".

Another challenging source of conflict will be related to values. The mission, vision, and values of your organization need to be clear and communicated consistently. Policies and procedures need to align with these values. Take any group of individuals, working together for any period of time, and their personal values will be on display.

Sometimes we don't live up to our own standards and values. Beyond that, we all have a bad day now and then. The trick for leaders I think at times, is to determine how to allow for that pesky humanness in ourselves and others, yet hold the line on foundational values.

Professional habits need intentional development, and sharpening from time to time. Conversations around conflict can escalate very quickly. How can you avoid contributing to that? Learn to give others your full attention, and give them the chance to release frustration and other emotions. Allowing for a pause after someone has really unloaded can help diffuse that situation. Many of us as leaders want to fix everything. I fall into that category. Wisdom teaches that *timing* is an important element related to the discovery of conflicts, and our responses.

Once conflict arises in a relationship, and certainly once you can confirm it exists, ignoring the friction and any incidences related to that is not the answer. Confronting conflict will be a growth area for most developing leaders, and most people for that matter. Whether at work, in life, even among friends and family, avoiding the conflict may be and feel like a sincere response. "I don't want to judge." Let's agree to disagree." "I'm afraid if I comment, it will only make it worse." Each of these are examples of inner dialogue we will wrestle with.

Unresolved conflict can spoil, damage, and destroy relationships. Avoiding or ignoring conflict could be perilous for you as a leader. Approach confronting with plenty of forethought, perhaps by outlining the objectives of a scheduled conversation with someone before it occurs. Leaders must learn how to get more comfortable over time, with uncomfortable situations.

Prepare questions in advance to work through a conversation where you decide to confront and get to the bottom of a conflict. Here are a few questions that may help. Do you see a way to come out the other side of this conflict in a good place with me? Or your colleague/s? How far back do we need to go to identify a conflict free relationship? What outcome are you hoping for, and how can we get there?

When a conflict is apparent, a team member may initiate a meeting with you. You may want to respond, in part, with questions like:

- What are you hoping to get out of this conversation? Are you looking to vent, or are you looking for resolution?
- Are you seeking advice or counsel from me?
- For any problems you will name, do you also have a potential solution?

If possible, attempt to discuss the nature of the conflict, including the origins, as opposed to the current position being taken by parties involved with the conflict. Fact finding helps. A lot of times, mis-communication and mis-understanding may be at the root of a conflict. Remember the intended / interpreted combination? Here is where that comes into play.

Often though, the ability to value and exhibit humility in some way can soften a conversation. Remember that. At the end of the day, leaders in whatever professional setting need to model and expect professional behavior. Patience and other critical character traits that most leaders are looking for in their followers, need to be mixed back into the mess of conflict. Admittedly, the space between avoiding an apparent conflict or confronting someone is filled with pot holes.

I used to tell my graduate students who were preparing to be leaders that no matter how hard we worked together in the classroom, much of what they needed could only be learned on the job. Make it a priority to work on your communication and conversational skills, especially in confronting conflict. If at all possible, get a mentor outside of your organization that you can count on to talk through related challenges. Role playing and candid discussions with a mentor prior to taking steps to confront could serve you well.

Communication, conversations, and conflict—the three C's. Keep them linked whenever you face challenges in relationships. As leaders, our integrity, trustworthiness and effectiveness of our communication are on display constantly. Our BELOW chapters have focused on these leadership essentials. How solid is the foundation of your leadership philosophy and style? Perhaps the *Integrity Switch* has motivated you to do some fine tuning to your approach as a leader.

Defining our foundational qualities is a start, but living them out is the ongoing challenge. What do we do then, when we fall down as a leader? Glad you asked. BEHIND is our next section, and that question will be explored in depth.

## Chapter Three Review

- Pay attention to your inner dialogue —"we talk to ourselves all day long".
- Place value on gratitude, loyalty, authenticity, and humility.
- All leaders make mistakes.
- Decisions impact others, and some of that impact will create conflict.
- Ensure that "why we are here" messages are crystal clear.

1 – What intentional communication approaches do you use?

2 – What pitfalls of poor communication have you experienced and made note of?

3 – How do you define a conversation? Any thoughts on "the conversation is the relationship" attributed to Scott's *Fierce Conversations*?

4 – Where are you on willingness to confront others, both personally and professionally?

5 – Did you underline, highlight, or star something in this chapter?

6 – Use the space below to design your ladder of success (see page 22). How many rungs will you have?

# ← BEHIND

Look back and you will get a sense of how far you have come. Isn't that what "once upon a time" is all about? Story telling should never become a lost art. A thoughtful look back is the only way to learn from the past. Reaching back and reflecting on lessons learned in leadership can provide a powerful perspective.

When we think about the vision of a leader, it's only natural to see that in terms of forward thinking. Vision might be linked to strategic planning, and moving ahead with new initiatives for the future. Visionary leaders often champion the importance of "seeing the big picture". Perhaps overlooked as part of that framework is a slightly different point of view—the value of hindsight.

The first two chapters in this section will provide many reflection points, including: discussion on blind spots, unpacking failure, and crisis management. You even get to see an example of a season long theme, that you may want to borrow to emphasize some powerful words. Chapter Six will highlight an approach to consider to recover from and avoid failure, and ends with a powerful pep talk.

# Chapter 4 – Blind Spots

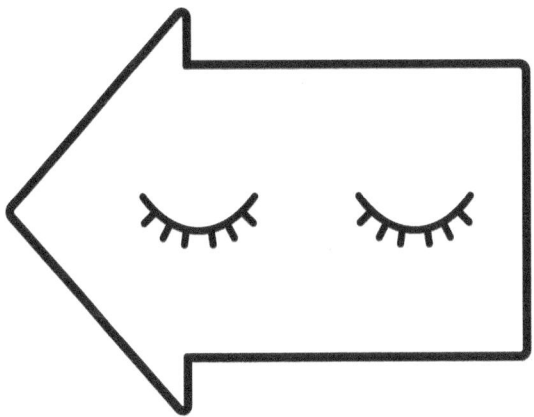

I have a healthy fear of lane changes when highway driving. Yes—fear of *my* lane changes. Despite checking the mirrors, I have had a few close calls as I started to slide over for an upcoming exit. Thankfully a couple of horn taps alerted me of someone in my blind spot. A quick, but careful swerve allowed me to avoid a collision.

What topics came to mind when you turned the page and saw this chapter title? Perhaps you plunged in here after thumbing through the Table of Contents. If so, were you recently blind-sided? Wouldn't that be another way of looking at this topic? Let's go back to the last time you said, "I didn't see that coming!" What made your scenario a surprise? Was it an unexpected departure of a valuable team member?

Perhaps, a budget revenue forecast for your current fiscal year was falling far short of expectations.

Predicting success is challenging in leadership roles requiring planning, executing the plan, and then assessing both the results and the process. We have all experienced unexpected surprises, or been caught off guard by a flaw in our planning that comes to light way too late. Building a new athletic facility comes to mind. Scheduling a number of site visits with a planning committee is pretty standard operating procedure. Having the chance to observe similar facilities to those you are designing allows you to see features you may not have under consideration. Most visiting committees generally arrive with one key question—"What didn't you think of?"

On a flight some years ago, I caught a glimpse of a newspaper headline in the hands of a passenger one row ahead—*Covid, Inflation Reveal Prediction Blind Spots*. I didn't find it surprising that those two topics might not be easily or accurately predicted.

How do we have blind spots in our bold predictions? High expectations might be a contributor. We narrow a candidate pool down to three finalists, and offer the position to someone we are certain will not disappoint. Then, they do. You might need to cut your losses, and open up the search again, but what if this becomes your pattern? Experience teaches us the value of due diligence when we are in the process of adding new team members. We dig deeper, and go beyond the list of references provided to ensure we aren't missing something. A sharp candidate should do their research as well. Often, the key in team building happens long before a contract is signed.

Coaches recognize the need for team building because roster management is one of the biggest challenges we face. The collegiate recruiting process centers primarily on one scary word—potential. The sport talent and athletic ability might be exceptional for our top prospects. Naturally, we have high hopes that these recruits can have an immediate impact, and often they do. Yet, the coach knows that only time will determine the ability of each newcomer to team with others. Just as importantly, a team culture must include a welcoming environment from veterans on the roster. If team cohesion is not on your mind all the time as a coach, that is probably a blind spot. The recruiting cycle is ongoing. Veterans including great peer leaders graduate, and new talent replaces them. Coaches may make this look easy, but guiding a program through annual roster changes can be a tough task.

The longer I coached, the more I enjoyed this challenge. I learned to pay attention to our first-year players in early practices, for signs of coachability. For some players, it takes time for them to stop playing for their high school or club coach, and start playing for you. Sure, I hoped every recruit was a great fit, and I think every recruit looks for a great fit, but team building starts with building each new relationship. The competition that lies ahead for every team will put a new player's attitude to the test. The daily grind behind the scenes gave me the chance to determine for myself the level of work ethic each player was willing to give.

Patience needs to be part of the process. Sharpening our observation skills helps, and not just during play. Often, I learned much more about each player and my team in the moments following a rally, especially when we lost the point. Coaches get to observe their team closely, and perhaps much more closely than you do in your team environment.

Might you have a blind spot in the recruitment and retention of personnel on your team? When was the last time you thought about the potential of your team members? Hopefully, your annual assessment and evaluation sessions provide ample time for discussion on this topic. The undercover bosses mentioned on page 13 stumbled on hidden abilities in some individuals they worked alongside of. Look carefully, and perhaps you will find some undiscovered talent on your team.

I have needed help finding some of my blind spots. Gaining insight on a regular basis from those you can trust, and those trusting you and your leadership, might help. When was the last time others were invited to help you discover a few? What aspects of your personality or leadership style might those reporting to you, wish you would change? I believe courageous leaders open up the opportunity and invite feedback at all points up and down the chain of command.

Possibly, you already have people you can count on to help you, especially when your vision is a little blurry. I was blessed to have that in my coaching. Now a retired USAF Brigadier General, Marcus Jannitto, was one of my men's volleyball assistant coaches at my first collegiate assignment. I wanted desperately to publish a coaching article. I was pretty creative and independent in my thinking even back then, but never believed any of my new drills to be worthy of publication.

We developed a competitive and successful program, very quickly. Early in our program history, we had a highly talented, but inexperienced, first year setter who was taking us to a new level. Despite his positive impact, our team was struggling with some of the decisions he was making on set point or match point. We had obtained a few multi-colored volleyballs that were new to the market for that season, and that gave me an idea. I designed a new drill where teams raced competitively through a long series of rallies with white volleyballs, to earn the chance to win the only point available with a single yellow ball, referred to as the *Bonusball.* I was convinced that my setter would "notice" that yellow ball and make better decisions knowing that was the only chance to score.

Proud as a peacock, I shared the new drill with the troops, and let them go at it for quite some time. What did I see? Predictably, our setter took every yellow ball and set it to our strongest hitter no matter what, which is not necessarily what we are looking for. Why? Because the other team is looking for that as well. So, dejected by another terrible drill, I blew the whistle, and sent the team for a water break. I walked over to Marcus, while literally crumpling up that part of the written practice plan, and tossing it in the trash. I will never forget the exchange. I was pretty steamed, and said, "Am I ever going to have an original idea worth anything in my coaching?" Marcus was all smiles, which I found odd since he had just witnessed a disaster. He responded, "What are you talking about"? I went on to say, "that is the worst setting drill I have ever seen." He quickly replied, "you are right about that, but that is the best defense I have ever seen our team play. Bring them back out here, do the exact same drill, and watch the defensive intensity".

The way the drill played out created extreme excitement on the court. As I watched the action with fresh eyes, the incredible effort by the players to keep the ball off the floor was in full display. What sold me was hearing, "Bonusball" screamed in unison by players on both sides of the net, when that ball was introduced for the final rally. Manufacturing that type of energy in practice is what every coach is looking for. I took a little stroll across the court, and pulled that drill diagram out of the trash can. *Bonusball* was published soon after.

## What If You Could Just Hit Rewind?

Sports fans have long ago expected instant replay to accompany big moments on a telecast featuring our favorite team. More recently, rule books have been revised to include conditions where a coach can issue a challenge for officials to take another look. The tennis elite playing at Wimbledon can also call for a review. As a result, a ball is ruled in or out by a fraction of an inch. Did you know that research results of human reaction time is built into the timing system for sprinters on the track, and is a factor in assessing a false start? This idea of looking back pervades the sports world, with a growing reliance on technology. The truth is—video doesn't lie. Unless the camera angle doesn't show conclusive evidence, replays are quite effective in assuring a correct call.

"How much are you willing to invest to be an effective leader?" For many years in clinic settings, I challenged coaches with that question to emphasize the importance of technology. Our teaching effectiveness is greatly enhanced when we can show an athlete a technical error. Video does just that. All too often, coaches begin to rehash a team's performance as soon as they finish the post-game handshakes. Experience teaches us that reviewing the video first, allows for a more objective and accurate perspective to share the next time the team gathers. The position I have maintained, and readily shared with coaches was, "You can't afford *not* to use video".

Our program made steady progress adding technology over the years, eventually obtaining TIVO for practice sessions. Our practices were videotaped with a 30 second delay, which allowed almost instant feedback for our players. Early in our practice sessions, our assistant coaches would work with a player performing a skill repetitively for 20 to 30 seconds, while I was stationed at our play back monitor. Each player would leave the activity, and immediately watch it back with me, and get specific skill feedback. Players could loop through this progression several times, using the observation and feedback in their next bout of activity.

We also gave permission for any players who rotated out of scrimmages to go right to the TIVO system and play back two or three minutes to watch their performance or ask an assistant coach to review it with them. We often stopped practice and took the whole team over to watch the last few minutes of practice, and you can imagine the mileage we got out of that.

My favorite memory was putting the spotlight on an unheralded player, after watching her make some great plays. I brought the team over when a long rally ended and said, "Watch Itza for this whole rally". She was a perfect model of a defensive specialist fulfilling all her responsibilities when she was not touching the ball. Her movement from and to each positional duty during our transition offense was amazing. She stayed low all the time. Her movement was efficient and purposeful. These were keys we had emphasized, and the video made her shine in front of everyone. I think Itza was like a lot of our team members, who may not have had the most impressive statistics, yet contributed greatly to our success. Every year, we honored an Unsung Hero at our team banquet for just this reason.

A later shift in our program culture included the use of computer programs that linked statistical tracking with video from competitions. What was the result? Eventually, if we had a two-hour bus ride home from an away contest, I could call the setter up to the front of the bus before the trip was over to sit with the coaches. We could click a few buttons and let her watch the 20+ sets she delivered to one of our attackers during the match that night. She could go home having already looked at her technique, along with the consistency of the location, height and tempo of her setting.

There are times when money can solve problems, and enhance effectiveness. The commitment to get the funding needed, and to train staff to utilize technology, enhanced the quality of our athlete's experience. How about your team? How can you hit the rewind button when you are assessing performance, and the contributions being made by individuals? What do you need to invest in to enhance effectiveness? Certainly, in the remote work environment that is rapidly replacing brick and mortar offices, technology is constantly evolving to allow owners to track the activity and productivity of workers. Augmented and virtual reality, and quantum computing are commonly identified as emerging technologies that will help businesses gain a competitive edge. Investing in these advancements likely will require securing new talent with skills and abilities to maximize their effectiveness.

## Unpacking Failure

We don't want to dwell in the past as leaders, but that doesn't mean we shouldn't pay it a visit. Leaders are typically eager to review and celebrate successes, but hesitant to take time to dissect failures. Yet, many inspirational stories center on bouncing back, or making a comeback. Numerous motivational cliches are offered to those who get knocked down. Many famous leaders openly tell tales of battles lost and hardships endured. Let's consider key elements that allow us to stare down failure.

For some time now, "Unpacking failure", is a phrase that began creeping into my seminars whenever I introduced blind spots as a topic.

Failure is inevitable when you step into leadership, especially when you are under pressure. Can you recall moments of heightened emotions where words you said were still hanging in the air when you realized you wanted to pull them back and re-state your last comment? I'm reminded of speech bubbles used in the comic strips. Conversations illustrated above the head of Lucy or Linus, greeted my childhood mornings. Sometimes failures in conversations become quickly apparent by the response we receive, and we want to grab those words back out of the air.

## Failure will find us.

As you take command of increasing responsibility and authority, the opportunity to fail increases. Fiscal and personnel management duties alone require constant attention. Leading projects, chasing initiatives, or enhancing your brand all include some risk/reward. You cannot expect to be perfect. Setbacks and disappointments will occur under your leadership, and how you respond to those matters.

Perhaps the first step in unpacking a failure is to look right at it. Show a willingness to review, discuss, and investigate what has happened. If possible, remain calm while sending a clear signal, that you want to understand where something went wrong. Keeping the focus on uncovering the facts will be much more productive than attempting to assign blame. When communication around what happened and why it happened is clear, and delivered directly to those effected, the impact of failure can be minimized.

Some leaders tend to be very tough on themselves, but the productive approach is to accept what has occurred as quickly as possible. In *Attitude 101: what every leader needs to know*, renowned leadership guru, John Maxwell shares, "Every successful person is someone who failed, but never regarded himself as a failure".[9]

Self-talk and inner dialogue were points of emphasis back in Chapter Three—those tools can be very helpful when discouragement sets in. Exchange wasted emotions like regret with positive thinking, and optimism that lessons learned from a recent failure will eventually strengthen your organization. Strong leadership requires resiliency, the integrity to admit mistakes, and the resolve to recover from them. Others will recognize and can learn from how you respond when times are tough.

Commonly we hear about the importance of, "Learning from experience". The reality is that some of those experiences will represent failure. Failure does not need to be fatal. Consider the spectrum of failure response descriptors positioned in the leadership scale below.

## Failure Response Scale

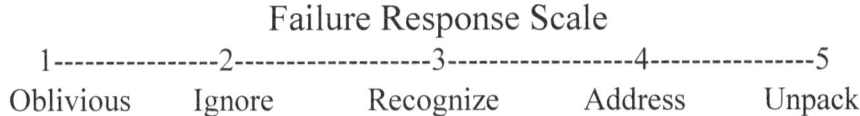

| 1 | 2 | 3 | 4 | 5 |
|---|---|---|---|---|
| Oblivious | Ignore | Recognize | Address | Unpack |

Earlier discussion on blind spots and feeling blind-sided are examples of how a leader can be *oblivious.* This seems like a harsh term, but the truth is there will be times when we are embarrassed and confounded by things we simply are unaware of. Effective leaders discover that *little things are big things.* Often, when something hits us out of the blue, upon reflection, we realize there were some signs along the way that we just missed.

Effective leaders don't overlook and *ignore* failures or problems, because that leads to compounding errors. Not every failure is a crisis, but turning a blind eye to a potential crisis will be costly. We will take a deeper look at crisis management in our next chapter, but bears noting here.

Effective leaders want to get things right. Recognizing that something has gone wrong, should provide motivation to explore all factors that have contributed to the current state of affairs. A strong team has members who are empowered to identify a problem when they see one. Some auto makers, allow those on the assembly line to stop production if they spot a problem. Regardless of how trouble is detected, making it clear that a significant issue has your full attention helps build credibility.

Addressing a failure represents the action phase. We may need to take immediate action. We have lots of tools available to us as leaders. We can suspend activity or pause a project. We can stop everything and bring all our stakeholders and team members up to speed. Leadership and problem solving go hand in hand. The "Growth mindset", that Carol Dweck introduced, happens one challenge at a time. As you lead action steps in recovering from failure, you will grow.

The concept of unpacking failure fits very nicely with a focus on the value of taking a look behind. Be sure you carve out time to carefully determine causes of failure. This will be time well spent. I mentioned earlier that I often developed a season theme as part of guiding our team through a season. Our next chapter will highlight a rather unique approach I stumbled upon when searching for a list of powerful words.

## Chapter Four Review

- Courageous leaders invite feedback
- The lost art of thoughtfulness may be the root cause for a failed decision
- Failure will find us.
- Failure does not need to be fatal.

1 - When was the last time you discovered a blind spot in your leadership?

2 - What do others see in you that you struggle to see in yourself? Why?

3 – What do you believe are the keys to being effective in your leadership role?

4 – How can you hit the rewind button to help your team members improve?

5 – Unpacking Failure – how do you find "the why" BEHIND something gone wrong?

# Chapter 5 – RE Words Like Remember

REmember, REspond, and REview. These are great examples of words starting with the letters "R" and "E" that fit nicely as we continue to look BEHIND.

RE words were at the center of one season theme, where each day, a new word was *revealed*, and applied in some way for the benefit of that team's season long experiences together. Powerful words like *responsibility, reputation, and recover* provide ample room for application, introspection or collective discussion.

*Remember* fits in so well with an arrow pointing back. Developing a good memory will prove helpful as you strive for consistency in your decision making, or enforcing *regulations*. *Record* keeping comes in handy when we can't *recall* details from a past event. Gathering information to settle a dispute or overcome some form of adversity will take time. Establishing a timeline that accurately *records* what happened, along with when and where events took place can be very useful. Label this working document as a draft, and update as needed as your *review* uncovers new information. Ask all involved who are working for a *resolution* to add their input. As you make progress, it is essential that the details around what has transpired are accurate.

This will be especially true during crisis management—our next topic.

## REcognize and REspond – Crisis Management

Hopefully as an *aspiring, developing, and emerging* leader you will have the opportunity to observe a veteran supervisor, or seasoned executive, handle a crisis before you need to. I have settled in over the years on two pieces of advice on this topic.

> Rule #1—know when you are in a crisis. Simple as that may sound—as leaders you don't have a moment to lose in handling a crisis. Not *recognizing* an incident or situation as a potential crisis from the outset immediately becomes part of how you handled the situation.
>
> Rule #2—when a crisis situation emerges, clear your desk, calendar, and schedule and begin the all-important task of gathering information.

Some of the thoughts shared earlier in *regard* to developing a timeline need to be implemented at this stage of crisis management. Perhaps the only thing worse as a leader than needing to handle a crisis, is the *regret* you may have in the aftermath, when it becomes clear that you mis-handled it.

Your integrity switch needs to be fully activated as *reality* sets in, especially if you find yourself in damage control. Integrity helps us *resist* any suggestions that promote some form of cover-up, or deception of any kind. Seeking the truth, and *reserving* judgment until all the facts are in hand, means we need to listen thoroughly to those with first-hand knowledge or involvement. However; there also are moments where you will be called on to discern and act wisely and decisively in the immediacy of some circumstances. Let integrity be your guide in answering that call.

Eventually you will want to develop a communication plan,. Determine who will communicate and who won't. Agree on what will be shared, script it out in writing, and then communicate precisely. If new facts emerge and as steps are agreed upon to *remediate* the situation, communicate those internally before sharing them externally. Professional *relationships* you have developed with experienced leaders will pay off when a situation *reaches* a crisis level. You will benefit from having wise counsel, and mentors available depending on how much information you are free to share.

In due course, the crisis will be over. Assessing damage, and evaluating the causes are all-important next steps. If not already in place, establish some form of debriefing as a standard operating procedure. Your core values need to be on display from start to finish, as you lead your team through a crisis.

*Recognizing* and *responding* to mis-behavior on your team or in your work setting might just prevent a crisis or two. Blatant defiance in following directions, disrespectful speech and actions, and failure to adhere to standard operating procedures, are behaviors that need a *response.*

There are also times as a parent, coach, teacher, and leader that we may choose to ignore a minor misbehavior so as not to *reinforce* it. This behavior modification is *referred* to as extinction. A teacher tells her third graders that she will be calling individually on students to answer questions. Before asking the first question, she adds that they are not to raise their hands. Of course, a good number of them do just that, with great enthusiasm. The teacher can help this go away, by simply not calling on anyone who is not following instructions.

Developing a list of descriptors to guide our *responses* may prove to be a worthwhile exercise. Informative, precise, and clear—perhaps even crystal clear, might top your list of communication objectives. How we *respond* will be observed, interpreted, and very likely passed on to others, especially when integrity is on the line. Finding and following the example set by a high character leader might be one of the ways we fine tune our integrity switch.

For years I taught a coaching principles class to undergraduates. I grew up in northern Maine in a town at the time that was best known for the paper mill, Mount Katahdin, and the high school basketball team. There was a bit of Hoosiers in the history of the basketball program, perhaps not unlike Milan High School, which is **reported** to be the actual town that movie was based on. Stearns High School of Millinocket won a number of State Championships and the 1963 New England Championship held in the Boston Garden. George Wentworth, a Notre Dame graduate, is the legendary coach who built and led the program.

Early in the semester, as the idea of having a coaching philosophy was emphasized, I used to **read** excerpts to the students from *Coach and his boys* by William R. Sawtell, who provided insight into the life and career of Coach Wentworth. [10] One story told of how he **responded** to basketball uniforms that were stolen from an opposing team. The **remedy** was telling the team there would be no more games until they were **returned**. He didn't back down, and the missing items showed up before the next scheduled game. In another story, a pie was taken from the display case of a diner in Bangor they visited after a contest. The owner was a good friend of the coach, and informed him of the theft before he left. The coach got on the bus and told the team, "I'll step off the bus and I want the manager to bring me that pie."[10] Within two minutes he did.

Coach Wentworth, like all leaders faced improper behavior that demanded attention. May we all be so fortunate as to have the challenges and problems we handle, be shared in the future as a model for others to follow. What a great way to be **remembered.**

## REview – As Simple As . . .Keep / Stop / Start

A good number of RE words have been highlighted already, but it seems appropriate to conclude this chapter with some thoughts connected to the value of **reviewing**. This leads us into the topic of evaluation and assessment. I believe personnel evaluations are meant to affirm, correct, develop, guide, motivate, notify and at times **reward**. We need to bring meaning to any process of evaluation that we may lead, whether it be annual *reviews* of team members and employees, or as discussed in Chapter Four, the process of unpacking failure.

I was evaluated annually as a coach by my supervisors and administrators. I was also *required*, late in our season, to establish a time when I would not be present, to allow my players to evaluate me. I certainly gained plenty of insight from all the feedback from those surveys, but I didn't stop there. In anticipation of one-on-one post season meetings to be scheduled, I asked my players to complete one more survey for me. I sent them a simple form with three columns labeled, Keep / Stop / Start. I was first introduced to this concept in the 1980's.

What a great way to lean into a *relationship*, by asking and being willing to *receive* feedback to the simple question, "What would you like me to keep, stop, or start doing in my interactions with you?" As you might imagine, the *responses* varied greatly, but I found them to be very helpful in those individual sessions. Usually, we started those meetings by *reviewing* the written individual goals each player provided during the pre-season. Once that was completed, I pulled out the survey they had submitted.

The *keep* items were encouraging to discuss, especially when the conversation *related* to communication between us, or aspects of our team culture. In many cases, the *stop* column was lengthy. Some of the objections were in *reference* to practice routines, or the physical demands of training. In Chapter Three (page 30), we discussed confronting conflict, and underlying tensions were often *revealed* in this category as well. Some great ideas emerged from *start* initiatives. I am certain that in some cases, the conversations sparked by using this simple tool, enhanced *relationships*. I designed the leadership scale below by inserting these three perspectives.

## Keep / Stop / Start Feedback Scale

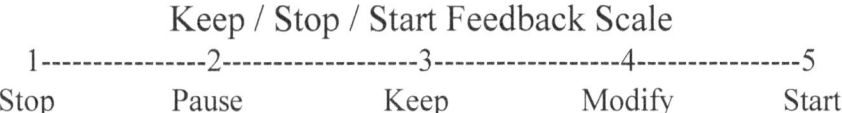

1----------------2-------------------3------------------4---------------5
Stop            Pause              Keep              Modify          Start

As you can see, I've added two descriptors that provide a few additional alternatives for leaders. Might a *pause* need consideration in **relation** to stopping? The trial-and-error approach might be useful as an intermediate step when consideration is underway to eliminate something. *Pausing* let's us experiment with that change, and better understand the implications, should we make a final decision to stop doing something. We could *keep* some things in place, but decide to *modify* them. A *modification* often is intended to improve something, but could simply imply adding or subtracting in some fashion.

A few other terms came to mind as I developed this scale. I had a dear friend who was quite fond of saying, "Full stop" at the end of conversations. This was usually delivered with extra emphasis and intended to be a conversation stopper. *Continue* is pretty close to *keep,* so you might prefer to swap those out.

This same scale can be helpful in our leadership in a few other ways. We could use Keep / Stop / Start to evaluate others, and benefit from the built in balance for our feedback. Everyone appreciates a slap on the back. "Keep up the good work", is a great way to praise or validate some specific areas of strength. You could use the feedback sandwich approach in organizing your discussion. Start and end by **reinforcing** the things you want someone to *keep* doing. This would allow you to slide the *stop* and *start* directives in between.

As leaders examine or evaluate their culture, these same terms might be applicable. I love introducing the following statement when challenging leaders on assessing their culture.

*If we always do, what we always did,*
*we will always get, what we always got.*

"Is that a good thing or a bad thing"? I believe there is more than one way to interpret this.

*Keep* or keeping seems to be one way of looking at this statement. "If it's not broken, don't fix it", could be appropriate—if business is always booming. That mindset can also **reflect** a blind spot. Just think of your local Mom and Pop shop that was a permanent fixture, perhaps even a community landmark, that closed their doors. An unwillingness to adapt when their competition added online purchasing, or delivery options might have been their undoing.

As we perform duties that *relate* to *reviewing*, we do need to define success, first for ourselves, and then for our team. We may be in a much better place to make decisions on what we need to *start* or *stop* doing, when we know what the *result* is that we are looking for. Be careful not to let others define that for you. When our team *returned* to campus after an away contest, we were always greeted by the same question. "Did you win?" The only people who first asked, "How did you play"?, were my coaching colleagues.

Of course, we valued winning, but our internal messaging was to have a championship mindset. Outstanding performances fueled by authentic competitiveness are needed to get to championships and contend for a title. We established a culture that valued the opportunity to improve daily. I believe our players benefited greatly from consistently training and competing with *realistic* but meaningful performance objectives established. We identified statistical and effectiveness levels of performance objectives around skills like serving, attacking, serve *receive*, and defense. We assessed our success both in practice and matches based on *reaching* those objectives.

Please don't miss that point. We won plenty of matches, but never lost sight of the objective of performing at a high level. Our players gained competitive maturity as a *result*. They could handle a "fierce conversation" when in *reviewing* a win, it was clear that our performance was subpar. Likewise, we lost some close battles, that included incredible performances. I still *remember* a superb defender setting a school record in a loss.

When was the last time you identified and/or *reviewed* the keys to success in your space? What metrics do you use? Most CEO's, heads of non-profits and other leaders are able to target success pretty effectively, but every team gets off track at times. Program and performance *reviews* are healthy and can *remind* us of previously established objectives that we may be falling short of. Lead your team in ***recommitting*** to the high standards you know are the keys to success.

By my count, nearly forty RE words made the final draft in this chapter. There is no shortage to the list of powerful words you can add to that total and incorporate in your work. Perhaps your goal in this chapter will be to come up with your own creative use of words that begin with "RE". This is the theme you are engaged in. So, follow the lead and get to it.

## Chapter Five Review

### CRISIS MANAGEMENT

- Know when you are in a crisis.
- When a crisis has been identified—clear your desk and schedule, gather information, and get the facts.
- Develop and execute a communication plan.
- Respond, then evaluate.

1 – *If we always do, what we always did, we will always get, what we always got.* Is that a good thing? A bad thing? True? False? Helpful? Not helpful? Explain.

2 - Choose 5 powerful RE words that can help you as a leader when you look back or BEHIND, with the goal of not repeating mistakes, and learning from failure.

3 - Remind yourself here of a time you were highly motivated by a *theme* that united a team of people, and it helped you achieve.

4 – What were your "take-aways" in terms of responding to a crisis?

5 – Does Keep / Stop / Start appeal to you as a tool to review? If not, what does?

6 – Who came to mind when you read about Coach Wentworth?

# Chapter 6 – Strengthening Strengths

We've discussed blind spots, and the importance of unpacking failures including crisis management scenarios. Plus, you are now armed with enough words starting with RE to fill up a monthly calendar. We need to learn from our mistakes and respond to them. But, we must not allow setbacks, or our own missteps to stop us in our tracks. Don't stop. Don't hide. Don't retreat. One way to get moving again is to turn your attention to what you do have going for you. Shift gears and take stock of your strengths.

Hopefully, you responded to the earlier challenge to identify your three un-mistake-able qualities. This provides a great starting point. Avoid focusing all your attention to improving, just on weak areas. What if the approach was not only to identify strengths, but to strengthen them?

Here's the coaching application. Pick a sport for a typical high school varsity coach, and it's likely their squad represents three levels of ability. It would not be unusual for 10-20% of the roster to be above average performers. We might call them the stars of the team. These players have the ability to perform well against exceptional competitors. They will challenge school records on the track or in the pool. A second group comprising 30-50% of a given roster, might be quite average in terms of talent. This group includes solid performers, along with less skillful individuals who possess strong athleticism. A dedicated veteran or two who lead by example, and are highly regarded by their peers may also be in this mix. Finally, there will be the last 20-30% of a roster that represent the future—the rising stars.

With such a wide range of abilities, the coach will naturally spend a high percentage of time with the average to below average performers. Those individuals are also guaranteed the opportunity to practice against or train with the team's top players. We may neglect the development and improvement of our best players very unintentionally. Don't forget to strengthen your strengths. Your best player or performer does not get to compete against someone better every day. Don't let this be a blind spot.

I remember one of my basketball coaches who challenged our starting five to break a pressing defense composed of seven teammates. Everywhere we turned there was a double team. Experiences like those reminded me to be creative in challenging the most talented players on my team.

Within the culture of a team sport or perhaps in your business, often the idea of strengthening our top performers is overlooked. When was the last time, you rewarded your top performer? Not with their name listed as employee of the month, but rather by stretching them to grow with an extremely challenging assignment? Following is an example of what that could sound like when you call an all-star into your office. "Jenny, your optimism is one of your greatest strengths. We have a new initiative, that some on our executive team are doubting. I want you to be on that team. This assignment will challenge you, but now is the time to put your optimism to work". There are also times when no explanation will be needed. When leadership positions become available, selecting an internal candidate sends a strong and supportive message to them.

Team leaders often spend less time developing our most reliable people, and much more time with underperformers. The failures and ineffectiveness of those struggling might result in shifting them to a new position. Another common response to those who do less, is to give them less to do, or less to be responsible for. Who picks up that slack? Our most productive and talented individuals get more added to an already growing list of expectations. Hiding and covering up for someone holding the team back rarely works out well. If no strengths emerge for a team member despite moving them from spot to spot, a tough personnel decision is probably on the horizon.

I think it is actually more challenging when a team member who exhibits a great attitude and work ethic struggles in their performance. While it is possible their strengths have not been identified, there is also the possibility they need to explore a different career option. Your influence as a leader for some team members may be temporary, but you might be the one who helps them move on. The leadership scale below has gone through a number of iterations, but I settled on this version to share. Experiences I had in coaching to strengthen our players and program are represented by the descriptors I selected.

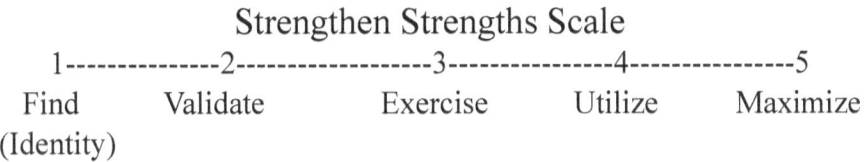

## Strengthen Strengths Scale

| 1 | 2 | 3 | 4 | 5 |
|---|---|---|---|---|
| Find | Validate | Exercise | Utilize | Maximize |
| (Identity) | | | | |

I loved challenging my volleyball players, nearly as much as I enjoyed challenging my own thinking. Blake Arena—our home court, had an unusually lengthy playing surface. Each endline is about thirty feet from the net, and a court is required to have at least six feet of free space outside of the boundary lines. Our court had nearly 30 feet of playable surface beyond each endline. This feature came to mind as a way to provide playing opportunities for some of our reserves, and create a home court advantage.

In successive women's and men's seasons, I remember talking to and working with some reserves who had very solid serves. I began to push them deeper and deeper away from the endline to initiate their serve. The players on the receiving end in practice struggled to adjust and handle serves now being launched much further away. In discussing this with the team, I reminded them that many opponents don't have home courts that allow them to prepare for this weapon. A handful of players worked their way on to the court by taking on this challenge. They took a strength, and made it stronger—to the benefit of our team.

Like many bright ideas, this one did not always play out as expected. Of course, when we went on the road, and played occasionally on courts with very minimal free space around the court, that weapon was taken away from us. My funniest memory of using a deep serve occurred with one of our men's players at Penn State University. That court had almost unlimited length available. Our server stood *so deep* on his serve, that by the time he sprinted to get on the court to play defense, Penn State had already drilled an attack to the area of the court he needed to defend. Of course, I made the mistake of glancing down the sideline at my friend—the opposing coach—who was looking my way, and getting a good laugh out of this. Made me chuckle too.

Trial and error. Weighing the pros and cons. Maximizing our strengths, and minimizing our weaknesses. All part of the learning curve as leaders. Challenge your own thinking, but pay attention to the results. Keep what works, discard what doesn't. What does it take for someone to be selected as an all-star? Their strengths are what get them to the *exceptional* level.

## Blending the Pieces

Developing and defining roles for all team members was a significant challenge as a coach. On the one hand, you want every player to crack the line-up. A team full of tough competitors who are driven in the relentless pursuit of earning a spot on the court creates a great practice environment. That same internal competition can also destroy team cohesion. We must uncover attitude flaws that will hold us back. Are you addressing team members who don't work well with others, or exhibit classic "prima donna" behaviors? That phrase reminds me of a very funny story. Years ago, a student in a coaching principles course, commented on this topic in a written assignment. The student mentioned the dangers of having a "pre-Madonna" on the team. These were my favorite moments when reviewing and correcting papers. I resisted the urge as I completed my grading, to write a note asking what that behavior was called before "she" came on the scene.

Teams with a strong bond are those where a team-first mentality prevails. Blending the pieces together in establishing a line-up was a major challenge for every season. There were a few exceptions to that, when we had a heavy presence of veterans returning from highly successful seasons. More typically, the first handful of matches gave us a good idea of what we had to work with, and how far we might be able to go with that particular team. Whether we had a set line-up that we did not anticipate changing, or found that we were juggling our lineup for every contest—we needed to be identifying roles for each player on our roster.

The hope was that teammates would recognize each other's strengths, and learn how to be supportive, in spite of coaching decisions on playing time. Often, there was very little separating three or four players competing for two spots in our lineup. I believed the players needed to hear that assessment. Leaders experience uncertainty daily, and sometimes a decision comes down to a "gut feeling". Understand . . . not all players will buy that, but working through disappointment and overcoming adversity are examples of life lessons that sports partic-ipation offers. Sometimes, the best we can do as leaders is to model how to communicate openly around tough decisions that impact others.

There is something else we can do as the season progresses. We can look for opportunities to, "Give someone a chance." That phrase was used often by Dad, when he shared stories of his coaching days. He would describe situations when he decided to provide a surprising opportunity to a non-starter. For me, these were stories about the human spirit. He reminisced about, "Seeing something" in a player who was not the best overall performer for a certain position. However, the strength he saw in that player was something that would fit nicely into the game plan for an upcoming opponent. Perhaps it was a physical trait like speed, or a specific skill that was particularly strong. I believe he accomplished a few things with this coaching style. Clearly, he raised hope in the minds of all players on the sideline, when he made these moves. I also think these unexpected changes inserted some well-placed reminders to the starters that they were always auditioning for their job.

In the business world, leaders work at creating a culture that people want to be part of. Referring to employees and staff as team members is a great place to start. Like you, I have heard the admonition to, "Get the right people on the bus, and get the right people in the right place". I hear less about how to do that. If you have not trained those you are leading from the outset of their careers, then you inherit their skills, mindset, and work habits. Which will be easier to spot, a weakness or a strength? Leaders need to evaluate both. Finding fault should not be the sole objective in a careful critique. Even as you discover areas that need improvement, commit to finding a strength or two for each team member. Effective leaders are able to accentuate the strengths and positives of those we are leading and marginalize their weaknesses.

Volleyball, like many team sports, features specialists. Our substitution rules allow us to exchange attackers and blockers, who play exclusively in the front row, with back row specialists, who we rely on for serving, passing, and defense. Perhaps, you are missing opportunities to mix some team members together from time to time to take full advantage of their combined strengths. Is cross-training part of your company or business? That strategy might help you uncover hidden talents, while also allowing team members to gain increased appreciation of the abilities of their teammates. You can imagine that attackers on a volleyball squad can become critical of their setters. To address this, I would occasionally have that attacker step in as the setter in practice. This "enlightening" experience generally resulted in a rapid attitude adjustment.

The assessment skills of coaches are tested constantly. Yours will be too. As you search for new talent, your ability to spot the strengths you are looking for, has everything to do with getting the right people. Your direct interaction with each candidate during interviews, must result in a clear understanding of the strengths they have confidence in. Evidence needs to support that when you follow up with strong probing questions to those they list as references.

When discussing team building on a zoom session with a handful of coaches, one participant started a sentence with, "Is a team ever, not better when . . . . ?" What a great question! As you have opportunity to add new pieces to your team, allow that question to remind you of exactly what your team needs.

Is a team ever, not better when the peer leadership is exceptional? I believe my most successful teams were the ones with great talent and great leaders. Part of the natural development for a coach is recognizing how to effectively empower those outstanding leaders. Before I probably knew how to spell empowerment, one of my players gave me a great lesson on that. In fact, as a young leader it was one of the best lessons I ever learned. There is no more powerful pep talk linked to my own coaching experiences that tops this one.

## A Championship Time-Out

My first collegiate volleyball post started back in 1981 when I was named the first varsity coach of a brand-new women's program. This program was initiated by students as a club and through their efforts, it became part of our intercollegiate athletic program. We had no home court. In fact, we practiced the first year in a local armory with cannons pointed at the court. Not kidding!

Fast forward to our 4th season and we found ourselves in our first regional championship match. We got there quickly, with some effective recruiting including a setter named Sharon, who was what I would call a gamer. A natural born leader and team captain, Sharon played well in practices, had tons of focus, but played her very best in matches. A gamer!

Back in that day, matches were still played as best of three, and your team only scored points on your own serve in games played to 15. Our team came out firing on all cylinders and took the first game, but lost the second, and fell behind pretty quickly in the deciding game. I called a time-out, and had just a few moments for what needed to be a highly effective time-out in this championship match. Our confidence was a bit shaken, and I decided to give a little pep talk as I pulled the team into a circle. As I was about to "instill" some confidence in the group, Sharon stepped into the middle of the circle, and for the first and only time in her career, she hijacked my time-out.

Sharon started with this, "Let me tell you exactly what's going to happen when we go back out there". She then stepped in front of our best blocker, and said, "Debbie, you are going to stop them at the net". Next up, she moved to her left and stuck a finger out at Pam and told her, "You are our best passer. You are going to pass every one of their serves right to my hands." "Wendy", Sharon continued, "every set I give you, you will pound it to the floor." Heidi was our spark plug reserve, and Sharon paused in front of her and said, "And you are going to cheer like you have never cheered before". Around the circle she went player to player, and finished with this, "and I am going to serve them off the court, and we will bring that trophy home".

There was a brief pause, and having been caught up in all the emotion, all the players finally turned and looked at me. Now, I only had a few seconds left in "my" time-out. This was quite a moment of truth for me, and somehow, and to this day I don't know where the wisdom came from, only three words came to mind that made any sense at all given what had just occurred. Attempting to smile with loads of confidence, I raised my voice a bit and said, "You heard her!" It seemed like they all grew an inch or two stepping out of that huddle. The rest of that game was not even close. I still have that photo of Sharon holding that plaque with everyone gathered around.

Sharon named their strength, looked them right in the eye and boiled it all down to one part of the game they were the very best at.

She focused on their strong points, and gave them an image of what the action would look like as they went back into the competition. So many lessons come from this story. Later in the book, when the focus is motivation or when I introduce the idea of standing in the gap, Sharon's leadership will relate to those topics as well. Enough trust and mutual appreciation had built up among the teammates, that when it was all on the line, there was something in this player that emerged.

Sharon has gone on to lead in her profession in amazing and impactful ways. None of that is a surprise to any of us who were part of her playing career. Sure, I have some other memories of time-outs where maybe I had an impact. My players certainly like to tell their favorite stories of my antics in time-outs and between sets. We all get a good laugh when reunion opportunities come along, and we share memories together. They embellish the impact of my double time-outs, and seem to recall all sorts of things I have long since forgotten. From my standpoint, and without exaggeration I may have been part of more than 5000 time-outs in my career, none stand above this one.

---

Never underestimate the value in accentuating the strongest skills, abilities, and talents of those you are leading.

---

Don't settle for outstanding when you evaluate your top performers. Keep working with them until they reach the exceptional stage. You will spend more time than you care to identifying weaknesses in your team members. In the midst of that, determine one or two strong points, and maximize those in ways that are in the best interests of your organization.

Time to move along from these *reflective* topics that represent BEHIND, and on to ABOVE. The hope is you will return to some of these concepts when a failure needs to be unpacked, or you suspect another blind spot needs to be uncovered. It is likely that as you gain experience as a leader, you will look back and recognize times you allowed yourself to be overly influenced, instead of trusting your instincts. You will have moments of truth that may require you to stand alone, at times based solely on principle. Your ability to grow through missteps may be what is needed to prevent you from dimming your *integrity switch* as you continue to encounter difficult situations.

Take note, that we did not "frame" failures, mistakes, or short-comings with a completely negative tone. We found powerful RE words to help us **recover** and **restore** our self-confidence for the next inevitable challenge. Strengthening strengths may have seemed initially as a strange topic to include in BEHIND, but I have found that way of thinking to be very powerful. We're not done with "framing", you'll see that for yourself as we turn our attention to things ABOVE.

## Chapter Six Review

- Strengthen your strengths.
- Effective communication is the key to helping team members understand their role.
- Never under-estimate the value in accentuating the strongest skills, abilities, and talents of those you are leading.

1 - What are your strongest.....

    ....character qualities

    ....abilities

    ....talents

2 – Have you ever completed a Strength Finders assessment? If so, what strengths were identified?

3 – What strategies do you use to blend the pieces in your team building environment?

4 - Is a team *ever* not better, when . . . . ?

5 – Do you have a favorite sports related pep talk?

6 – How do you define empowerment?

# ABOVE ↑

The team, seated in the locker room, expected a fiery speech from the coach, before they charged on to the field for the title game. Instead, they heard these words, "I have just one word to say to you today. You need to listen very carefully to the instructions you are about to receive, and make sure you comply fully."

The coach paused, then swiftly and forcefully demanded, "Everyone, lift your hand as high as you can!" Just as quickly, the hands shot up. The coach allowed just a few moments, then shouted, "Higher!" Shoulders extended and indeed, hands elevated. "Higher!", the coach shouted again. Players began to stand, some on tip-toes, and one last time they heard, "Higher!" Players jumped on the benches, some jumped in place until the coach finally said, "I told you the first time to lift your hands as high as you could, but every time I said higher, we all saw your hands climb in the air". Pausing one last time, the coach finished with, "What do we need today out there? Higher!"

Just one problem with that "pep talk" for high school or college coaches. You can only use that every four years for full effect, and to ensure no player has experienced it before. I can't think of a better way to introduce ABOVE then with the concept of *higher*. Reaching higher, raising the standard, aiming high, elevating our performance, moving up, and looking up —all are lofty and inspirational concepts. For me, and perhaps many reading along, a faith-filled prayer lifted ABOVE could be the best place of all to start your work each day.

Are you able to re-frame an issue for yourself? This will be our lead-off topic in this section. The value for leaders to think independently, and trust their instincts will be part of that discussion. The entire focus of Chapter Eight is change. You'll walk through a seven-step outline that can be helpful when change is needed to bring your team to higher heights. The following chapter will focus on confidence— the importance of developing self-confidence, instilling confidence in others, and gaining the confidence from those you are leading will be highlighted topics.

# Chapter 7 – Re-Framing

"Keep your head up" is usually delivered with sincerity from those who care about us as we encounter adversity. If your head is up, your eyes can look up. Even the most seasoned daily freeway commuter can be caught looking up, when an over-arching rainbow suddenly fills the sky. Motorists often find a safe place to pull over hoping to capture a panoramic view photo to catch the full perspective.

When was the last time you edited a photo by choosing the crop function? Likely, you were swiping from multiple snapshots of the same scene, and looking for the best of the bunch. Perhaps the grandparents have requested a birthday party head and shoulder shot of a young guest of honor, destined for a 5 by 7 frame. Or, you may have taken a rapid series of sunset photos at the beach. As you review them, you are looking for the distant catamaran to be perfectly centered in that orange ball sitting on the ocean horizon. You noticed I hope, that when you hit the crop button, your images were framed. The best selfie of you with your small group, may need re-framing, if only to get your finger out of that top left-hand corner.

The house flipper buys a ranch but envisions a second story re-framing project. The pitch of the roof is changed, a staircase goes in, and living space gets added. To add even more value, a few interior walls are removed, load bearing beams are installed, and a new "open concept" emerges on the first floor. Re-framing results in expanded square footage, and increased investment value. How leaders think independently enough to frame and/or re-frame issues for themselves, can certainly add value to a team.

Lots of inventions came to life because something didn't work or seemed to make little or no sense. The solution arrives with a new device, a new approach, or a completely new way of looking at things. Dick Fosbury flopped backwards, initially the only high jump competitor at the time to do so, when he discovered and utilized the technique named for him. Of course, saw dust pits quickly became outdated, and foam landing pads were adopted. Fosbury's insight of a better biomechanical strategy to get his center of gravity safely over a fixed point revolutionized this event. Our leadership and how we bring ideas into our boardrooms, our staff meetings, and our team practices require the same type of deep thinking, and an open mind for change.

A paradigm shift is defined as a *fundamental change in approach.* That definition is a little ironic as it relates to the high jump. However, Fosbury's key adaptation was not just in running towards the bar—*the approach phase*—but obviously in clearing the height with a radically different idea. Re-framing, like a paradigm shift, can simply be another way of looking at things.

Let me share an example of re-framing that resulted in a significant team culture change in how we selected and trained captains. The need for the change started when I noticed that some of my senior captains were not performing up to their capabilities. I think I may have been like a lot of coaches. While not intentional, I was handing a good deal of team drama, along with internal tension issues, over to the captains to handle. I was likely unaware of additional team dynamic challenges that the captains were already dealing with.

A theory emerged that perhaps my captains were distracted by these leadership assignments. I also realized that I wasn't preparing our captains to handle team turmoil. The result was becoming apparent— their performance was being diminished because our matches did not have their full attention. The changes implemented over the course of a few seasons included new procedures for selecting captains, assigning specific roles for each one, and conducting formal training to prepare them for that role.

Key adjustments we made included:

- Engaging returning players to identify the peer leadership skills they felt would be most beneficial to the team for the upcoming season.
- A new self-nomination tradition emerged. To self-nominate, a player had to step forward and identify the role they pledged to contribute as a captain. "I will lead by example on and off the court every day", was one of my favorites.
- The players voted from among those who self-nominated. The ballot listed the peer leadership skills the team valued, and the intended role of each nominee.
- I designed a formal training program for those selected with a focused emphasis on when and how to effectively lead in their publicly announced role.

I am big on traditions; you may be as well. A closer inspection of the role of team captains, identified one key missing piece—captains often receive little or no training for that role. I never really stopped tweaking the process, but in retrospect, I am confident that our culture was enhanced by the change. Our captains were better prepared for the specific role they had accepted, and I made sure not to add additional pressures. Most importantly, our veteran players in leadership roles were less distracted, and better able to focus on performance.

Over the years, in conducting coaching clinics, I would ask the coaches two related questions. First, I would ask, "How many of you served as a team captain?" You could expect 75% of the hands to go up. The follow-up question was, "How many of you participated in formal training for that role?" Sometimes no hands were raised. This is probably a good example of a blind spot. *Follow the leader: Beyond Captain Selection* was published in 2012. A full account with lots of detail is available there that recounts the work we did in re-framing the work of captains on our team.[11] You'll be asked in the chapter review section to comment on something in your organization that may need to be framed in a new way. Be thinking about that.

One *Merriam-Webster* definition of *outside of the box thinking* is "to explore ideas that are creative and unusual and that are not limited or controlled by rules of tradition".[12] That may be the phrase you prefer to use to describe creative thinking. What I discovered along the way is that I needed two related tools—first, the ability to frame an issue, challenge, or initiative, and secondly the willingness to re-frame how any of those may be presented to us.

Leadership styles provides a nice example for consideration. Common perceptions of leaders might include a wide array of descriptors—demanding, charismatic, aloof, perhaps even unapproachable. Authority figure comes to mind to fit that style of leadership. When the leader is described as personable, encouraging and collaborative, the image of a leader changes dramatically.

To some degree, we may all be a little programmed in what we might expect from a leader. From, "Taking charge to taking credit", our experiences and stereotypical images of leaders we encounter will influence us. Let's look at a leadership approach that may feel counterintuitive if it has not been modeled for you.

## Servant Leadership

Of all the leadership theories out there, this one seems to fit best when talking about re-framing. The phrase, Servant Leadership, was coined by Robert Greenleaf.[13] If we think of leadership as top-down, with a chain of command image in mind, this approach turns that model upside down.

> A servant leader makes it a priority to serve those they are leading.

I was helped immensely as a Director of Athletics early in my career, by my environment. Most of our head coaches were part-time. I insisted that our full-time staff, do all that we could to serve as "unofficial" assistant coaches to this group. After all, these program leaders were often rolling into the parking lot at 2:55 for a 3 pm van or bus departure. Long before iPhone applications became available, the coaches needed travel directions, especially if they were driving a van. They were also relying on us to have their meal money, equipment and uniforms ready for pick-up. All of this would be after they had likely reported to their full-time job at 7 or 8 A.M.

I'm sure our coaches needed more assistance than we sometimes provided, but I know they appreciated every effort our staff made on their behalf. We developed a service mindset to meet some specific needs. We also valued opportunities to meet needs within our community. Providing or responding to volunteer opportunities is a great way to serve others. How can you place a new or renewed emphasis on volunteering within your organization?

My favorite ice breaker for a workshop is to open with, "I'm looking for a volunteer." Usually, there will be no immediate response, especially if these are my first words after being introduced. I remain quiet and relaxed, and wait patiently for a response. Eventually, someone speaks for most of the group by saying, "Well, what would I be volunteering for?" My quick response is, "You'll have to volunteer first to find out." Regardless of how the first responder emerges, I ask the person to come to the front of the room, and let them know they volunteered "To receive a gift". While holding up a nice hardcover leadership book—I'll show the group that I have already written inside the front cover the following words, "Don't ever forget the value of volunteering." I add the recipient's name to the top of the message, and generally remind the group that, "Serving others is at the heart of volunteering."

Servant leadership certainly has some spiritual roots as well, which reminds me to comment on one other topic—the idea of sabbath. Yes, I mean the principle of resting. I'm sure you have noticed that leadership can be all-consuming. The "to do" list gets chopped down, but will never be empty. There will always be another task available for you to tackle, or a problem to solve. How about this? I am going to ask you to stop for about 30 seconds for an activity. Ready? Take a moment to get comfortable, then inhale slowly through your nose, hold it for a second, then exhale slowly through your mouth. Repeat this five times. When was the last time you did that?

We push ourselves as leaders, much more perhaps, than we realize. I want to encourage you to put some boundaries around your time, and plan for a time of rest. This is not ground breaking advice, but we all need to make it a priority to take care of ourselves. Perhaps you do a great job with this already—kudos to you if that is the case. For many leaders, this is not the norm. While never my own strong suit, I can remember the value, when an intentionally planned break really made a difference for me.

Does someone come to mind when you think about servant leadership? Mark Sanborn's *The Fred Factor: How passion in your work and life can turn the ordinary into the extraordinary* is a must read if you will be leading in a service-oriented environment.[14] Fred is a mail carrier who has a remarkable impact on those he served. While he makes it look easy, he seems to go above and beyond any reasonable expectation on a daily basis. He knows his customers, and he makes himself known by how he finds ways to be of service.

Why is our household loyal to a realtor, a plumber, an electrician or our favorite tile specialist? How they handled themselves before, during, and after delivering a service has an impact on us. Most of them arrive to meet us, just after leaving another customer— perhaps one who has turned complaining into an art form. The professionals we welcome back have the ability to show up ready to answer questions, offer advice, provide quality work and stand behind it. Plus, they actually thank you for your business every time you hand them a check.

A concern for others displayed by compassion and empathy, and a willingness to put others first—both of these will be observable in servant leaders. How can you make those "others oriented" qualities observable in your leadership?

I want to offer one more perspective that relates to re-framing how we look at things—this one may be a bit more *uncommon.*

## Uncommon Sense

"If you know what makes sense and what is nonsense" was part of the hidden gem that I found in the letter (described on page xxv) from my father. The straightforward advice, provides yet another leadership scale to consider. The two foundational phrases, "What makes sense?" and "What is nonsense?" provide two concepts to juxtapose.

Dwell on this for a minute. Imagine a father thinking back, possibly over a life time of leadership experiences, and boiling it all down to one solid piece of advice. Study the admonition again and read between the lines. "Son, you are going to hear some nonsense!" This was both a well-informed prediction and a warning. In heeding this advice, I've learned to ask myself, "What makes sense?", or simply, "Does this make sense?"

## Uncommon Sense Scale

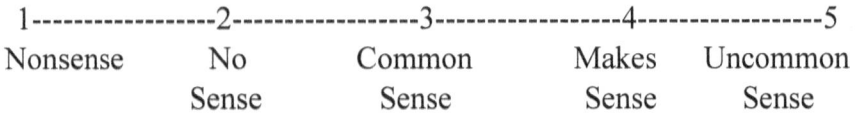

| 1 | 2 | 3 | 4 | 5 |
|---|---|---|---|---|
| Nonsense | No Sense | Common Sense | Makes Sense | Uncommon Sense |

I worked on this scale for years, until one day the idea of *uncommon sense* popped into my head. Dad took on many leadership roles within his profession—he was a leader of leaders. In fact, after his retirement, he was involved in the formal mentoring of many educational administrators. I treasure that letter, and *this is by far* my favorite leadership scale. I was guided by Dad's advice for decades, and took full advantage of his wisdom throughout my years as a coach, a teacher, an administrator, a husband and father.

I continue to toy with the Uncommon Sense scale that I attribute to him. When you facilitate discussion within your inner circle of leaders, this scale might be helpful. Sadly, some leaders intentionally pitch *nonsense* to their followers. I hope you won't follow that example—your integrity will be compromised if you do. Learning to detect *nonsense* should motivate you to re-frame an issue or situation for yourself. As you review this scale, consider the differences between nonsense and something that makes *no sense*. You have probably been with someone who has *no sense* of direction when they are traveling. Relying on a mobile application to get from point a to point b can be highly effective, but that "app" is of little use when your phone battery needs replacing. You may also have someone you care about who appears to have *no sense* of direction for their life.

*Common sense* has to be on this scale somewhere. We get lots of "this type" of advice as a kid about chewing our food before swallowing, keeping our hands away from the stove, and not stirring up the hornet's nest under the patio stairs. Often, we just need *common sense* to make a choice or a decision that *makes sense.* As you begin to gain leadership responsibility, learn to go beyond identifying something that *does not* make sense. Be ready to suggest solutions of what would *make sense.*

I continue to be intrigued with the idea of *uncommon sense*, and bringing meaning to that from a leadership standpoint. Are the great military commanders down through history, studied and copied because they had *uncommon sense*? Perhaps. Is uncommon related to unique or the ability to think and plan and execute so effectively that uncommonly positive results emerge? Possibly. For example, history reminds us of out-numbered armies winning the day because of uncommon thinking and leadership.

One *uncommon approach* I used that involved re-framing makes for a good transition to our next chapter where the topic is change. This story is also an example of how to recover from making a mistake. After a highly competitive men's team selection process one season, and despite having perhaps my deepest talent pool of all time on my roster, I started getting a nagging feeling. Our team was missing something. The chemistry wasn't right, and I just kept picturing this one first year player, who had a contagiously positive attitude. Our team needed someone just like him, and I kicked myself for not seeing that when he narrowly lost out on a roster spot. When the season ended, I decided to do something about my error. I sent him a note and asked him to stop by the office. I asked him if he would join my camp staff that summer. Despite a few awkward moments, I added, "Listen, I really want you to try out again next year".

Fast forward to tryouts, my invitation was accepted. This talented team needed some attitude adjustments. I let all the candidates know we had some new practice shirts coming. On the first day of practice, I found the most ancient, squeakiest, portable garment rack available to pull in to our practice area. Fifteen shirts on hangers were displayed right there in the gym. The shirts had great historical meaning attached to our institution, but they were anything but flashy. A few of the guys, a bit underwhelmed, had some negative comments about the shirts. I repeatedly said the same thing, "Oh, I think you are really going to want one of these shirts".

I let the first practice go on for quite some time, just waiting for this young man to display great effort and attitude in pursuit of a ball that would be evident to all. As he was scraping himself off the floor following a great save, I blew the whistle sharply. "Circle up every-one", I shouted, as I went over to the shirts and ripped one right off the hanger. I called this young man's name out and told him to step into the middle of that circle. I packed that shirt up in my hands like a snowball and threw it right into the middle of his chest, and said, "Congratulations, you have made this team, now put that shirt on." One of the best responses to my own failure that I can think of. Yeah, there was suddenly a whole new interest in those shirts as they came off the hanger one at a time over the next few days.

I had never forgotten my junior year in high school, when I got shirt 11 of 12 that came out of a bag my basketball coach brought daily to tryouts. In all my years of coaching, I used that procedure just this one time. There was no cut list that year. Team selection was re-framed for everyone to see, one pick at a time. I like parts of this idea, and other parts not so much. I'm not advocating coaches that you use this, rather see how powerful re-framing can be. Sometimes, things just need to change. More on that topic coming up.

## Chapter Seven Review

- Re-framing, like a paradigm shift, can simply be another way of looking at things.
- A servant leader makes it a priority to serve those they are leading.
- Put some boundaries around your time, and plan for a time of rest.
- Leaders are able to determine the difference between what makes sense and what is nonsense.

1 - Do you recall a missed opportunity in re-framing a topic of discussion that would lead to a decision?

2 – What does servant leadership look like or mean to you?

3 – Reflect with a comment or two on the phrase "Uncommon Sense"

4 – How can you re-frame this scale and make it your own?

## Uncommon Sense Scale

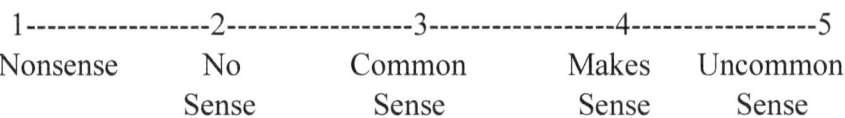

| 1 | 2 | 3 | 4 | 5 |
|---|---|---|---|---|
| Nonsense | No Sense | Common Sense | Makes Sense | Uncommon Sense |

# Chapter 8 – Change

There is no shortage of enlightening quotes you can search for on the topic of change. Insights will include how change is inevitable, healthy, and opportunity laden. As a leader, you must constantly survey the landscape in your field of expertise. Best practices and benchmarks, that represent changes to standard operating procedures in our industry may influence our thinking in terms of some changes we should at least consider.

What are the key functions of a leader? Generally, administrators as an example, will need to be prepared for six essential functions: planning, organizing, leading, implementing, controlling, and evaluating. Most of these functions probably apply to CEO's, managers, and a good assortment of other leadership roles.

ANTICIPATING CHANGE
This is our stepping off point. When I think of anticipating change, I am reminded that time is needed to determine if something new is a trend or a fad. Effective leaders need to pay attention to trends within their own companies, and externally in the competitive market. Our competition gets our attention when they make a strategic change. There is an element of risk/reward as you recognize signs of change and consider when and if to move some part of your organization in that direction.

Technology certainly comes to mind. As consumers, we have seen significant change simply in how we pay for a purchase, whether that be a product or service. Business leaders in a multitude of industries can easily recount, when and how often they needed to make changes in this area. In some instances—timing "is everything". Some good questions might be: What could happen? And also, what will happen? Effective leaders take the time to determine whether current success and/or recent successes are effective indicators for what is to come.

How do we keep our critical thinking caps on as we focus on today's challenges? Is our team built to last? Are we surviving or thriving? The following statement was introduced in Chapter Five— "If we always do, what we always did, we will always get, what we always got." I can't remember where I first heard this, but I am obviously enamored by it. How does it relate here to the topic of change? Is the statement true? If yes, then how so? A part of me likes the idea of building on what has worked in the past, and that part of the statement resonates with me. On the other hand, we must recognize that change will occur and that our goals and objectives and the metrics used to measure success may need to be adjusted. I also can see it as a call to action. Do we settle for status quo? Probably not if we are in need of innovation or improvement.

## Planning, Challenging, Leading

PLANNING FOR CHANGE in your organization or company may include succession planning. This may be an uncomfortable topic of discussion for you, especially if you aren't the one bringing it up. Dad told me a good number of times to "Get out of coaching before they want you to". Perhaps you can benefit from that advice in some way, if only to consider for the first time, how do you want to go out?

If you are the leader in your organization, perhaps consideration needs to be given as to how you want others to go out, or advance. There are many reasons that I have great admiration for the YMCA organization. The historic roots and ties to my alma mater are very meaningful to me. In the context of this topic, I have not seen an organization more intentional on career advancement of their professionals.

Professional development needs to be more than programming. Assisting young professionals in their climb is an example of planning for change. How did you advance to where you are in your career? Most likely, you have had some assistance along the way. I listened to a highly successful coach once, who commented briefly upon receiving a very prestigious award. The message was simple. "How did I get here? How does a turtle get on a fence post?" Think about it!

## Plan the work → work the plan.

This is one of my favorite guiding principles, and it applies nicely to the idea of planning change. When we take time as leaders to plan, it usually does pay off. Discipline will be a key ingredient in following and working through the plan. This concept can be applied to how you lead yourself—both on a daily basis, and also in your career planning.

As *aspiring, developing and emerging* leaders, you may be on the verge of a career move. Recently, I was able to observe a young professional completely change his career path. This was a well-thought-out change. Your career moves also need to be carefully calculated. At the same time that he was assessing several years of work in one field of expertise, he was thoroughly researching a completely different industry that he sensed was calling his name. He made a series of committed decisions that required investing in himself. As he juggled yet another educational degree, in pursuit of his dream, he was developing the skills and expertise he would need. Yes, it did pay off. Within two years, interview requests began to arrive and eventually the job offer came. He transitioned smoothly. Leaders, do you get caught by surprise with these types of career moves from members of your team? We all respond differently to change.

Perhaps you can relate to the following process of change. My bank went through a merger, and I decided to take the journey with them. To their credit, the slew of communication I received seemed endless. Step by step instructions were provided to help me anticipate the experience I was about to have as a client. I needed to rip up all the old checks including the new batch I had just paid for. Then, I waited for the transition period when eventually I would receive my new personal and business account numbers. By necessity, I then needed to update all my auto payments, plus that bank held our mortgage, so that required some attention too. Within two years, while making a deposit at this bank, I received a courtesy announcement from my teller that the bank would be going through another acquisition and change in the next twelve months.

Despite effective planning and communication, people interested in the outcome will have their own opinion. This is inevitable. My response to staying for the second bank merger was, "No thank you. I am not taking that ride again." Now—that is just one client's response, but the point is that even with stellar communication, not everyone is going to go along with change, or keep going along with change. Place value on the planning phase, and consider the likely objections. Stand in the shoes of those who will be impacted. Prepare your clients, consumers, members—all who will be affected.

CHALLENGING CHANGE

There is a time for debate and a time for decisions. That is probably the order in which change should occur. The idea of allowing for discourse, dissent, and push back was explored earlier in Chapter Two, and those thoughts can be applied here. One of the key characteristics of high performing teams is shared vision. In-depth and respectful conversations are critical. Most groups who carefully weigh the pros and cons of significant changes, can end up on the same page. Does your leadership team allow for challenging questions? What does that look like, and how do you develop that? Start by setting time aside to fully explore, and identify all the questions that need to be asked *before* arriving at a decision.

What would be my goal? That the participants in the discussion/s would describe the conversation as lively, and inclusive of opposing and dissenting voices. I would hope that the group dynamic would not be characterized as leader dominated. Pay attention when you realize that is you. How will you know? Simple. You are the one doing all the talking while your executive team members all stare straight, ahead and nod in agreement.

I was blessed with some long-time assistant coaches, who rarely wasted their breath on agreeing with me. I knew they did agree, when they had nothing to say. On the other hand, many three-minute inter-missions between sets in our matches were spent several feet away from the team in our own little circle. Those discussions included some pretty good debates about what, if anything, needed to change. When you have dedicated personnel, invested in the mission and in your organization, you will learn to trust good advice. When the leader chooses a course of action, not suggested in that inner circle, those who assisted with advice will at least know they were heard. Gratefully, our staff never operated with an "I told you so" attitude.

I should add that it was pretty neat when staff longevity resulted in simple collaborative decisions. My college teammate and long-time assistant—Coach Lynch—was a good example. Often, when I was internally debating on taking a time-out, I would turn and look down the bench at him. Generally, he was already squared up and staring straight at me. That is what you call, "Confirmation."

## LEADING CHANGE

The decision for change has been made. The debate needs to be over—at least for now. Down the road, and this chapter will close with this topic, it will be important to evaluate the effectiveness of that change. For now, the key leadership moment of truth is to get out in front and lead the change. People are watching, especially your critics. The impactful leader will need to champion and to identify with the change.

I can recall when a guest speaker made this point to my students in a discussion on re-branding. This Director of Athletics reviewed a recent campaign to re-brand an intercollegiate program at the Division I level. The presentation provided insight on the process, all the constituents involved, and the financial impact. The speaker placed a great emphasis on the period of transition, and the significance of leading by example in those moments. The leadership team, without exception, wore only new gear sporting the new logo. They insisted that all coaches and student-athletes do the same, and enforced that policy consistently. The speaker was candid in sharing the challenge of having an entire community embracing such a change. Positive and consistent messaging from the leaders, along with creative marketing and promotional efforts, were keys for the new brand to quickly be embraced.

As you are leading change, develop two or three talking points ready to reinforce why this change is occurring. Announcing the change internally before it goes public or to external audiences is important. For a small business, this could be as simple as a lunch time gathering of all personnel. In college athletics, press conferences are scheduled to announce the new coach or director of athletics to the public, and in some ways there will be both internal and external audiences. The point here is to be intentional in how the change is announced.

When you are in the run-up phase for a change to be initiated, this is a great time for increased visibility, and perhaps availability as a leader. You and your leadership team will benefit from listening, and gathering the list of concerns constituents are expressing. As opportunity presents itself, leaders can share those openly and respond if possible to some of the concerns.

Experience in leadership roles teaches us the dos and don'ts of how to lead in so many different situations, and leading through change will be one of those. Make note of lessons learned in the past, seek out mentors for how best to lead change, and then step up and lead.

# Implementing, Managing, Evaluating

## IMPLEMENTING

Some professional experiences related to this topic relate very well to blind spots discussed back in Chapter Four. Let's talk about the phrase, "Effective immediately". I get it. A new law is passed or a crisis occurs where your risk management plan now needs an adjustment. There are times, when policies or procedures or other measures need to be effective immediately. Unforeseen and unique events occur, and they require a response.

However, as decisions for change are made, there are also situations where the timing of implementing change must be taken into consideration. As leaders, we need to keep a careful eye out to avoid making a change that in any way undermines the integrity of the organization or an individual in the organization. That could be a blind spot.

Let's say that an employee makes a commitment to a customer, and in doing so, is simply following a current standard operating procedure. Your salesperson has confirmed and placed an order for a customer. The customer has a purchase order from your company with a date on it. Most devoted customers will hang in there when informed of a delay. How would you expect that customer to respond when shipping *has always* been included on all items over $5000, then suddenly—their bill includes a shipping fee? Will they "buy it" when your salesperson apologizes and informs them of this new policy—effective immediately? That type of implementation places customer satisfaction in jeopardy.

Many engineering or construction projects go through careful planning and eventually detailed timelines are produced. Perhaps a timeline of sorts would be a useful tool to develop for significant change you are leading. As the timeline takes shape, communication details will start to be included, and if a policy change is involved, the implementation of that change will be shared.

Using a sports analogy, major league baseball enacted a clock for both batters and pitchers for the 2023 season. Everyone knew the implementation date in advance. Sportscasters shed light on the change months in advance. Behind the scenes, in anticipation of the implementation—managers, coaches and players— were all preparing to make adjustments. A timeline evolved in this case, that was healthy. Leaders of the sport had done some trial-and-error experiments with this change, and eventually settled on the specifics. For a few weeks, enforcement of the new rules had a few wrinkles that needed to get ironed out, but before long, most everyone just settled in.

In summary, establish a communication plan that prepares all stakeholders for impending changes, especially policy changes. Remember to avoid, if possible, allowing the implementation timing to damage the integrity of your team members, and be the champion of the change.

MANAGING CHANGE

One of the unique aspects of being a college coach is the reality of annual changes in your roster that impact your recruiting targets. Talent acquisition and talent development go hand in hand. Often, we were developing a replacement for next year's starting line-up from within, while at the same time we were attempting to solve that challenge with a high impact recruit.

Many organizations have procedures in place both for internal candidates and external candidates. Working through a search process that features both current team members or employees, competing against prospects looking to join the team is tough work. For the internal candidate and those at the supervisory level, this process can be painful. Communication will be key for all those involved. The last thing we want is to lose a valuable team member who applies alongside external candidates for a new position, and leaves the organization if not selected.

What are the stresses and strains of retention that you are facing with your work force? We never really know when someone is going to give their notice, right? Anticipating personnel changes by investing heavily in cross training, or routinely increasing responsibilities to your rising stars can come back as a huge benefit when hit by unexpected staff exits.

## Take care of your people.

We read about and discover very successful companies who espouse this philosophy. The underlying strategy centers on the idea that a happy workforce will shine through in their daily efforts, and customers will be impacted positively as a result. As a coach, there will be no greater ambassador for your program, then those on your roster or your alumni. As leaders, we need to truly care for our people. Is that approach clearly evident in your culture?

Despite our best efforts, we will be disappointed and surprised by some departures. My collegiate coaching ended before the NCAA transfer portal was established. Name, image and likeness (NIL) incentives for athletes was still in the debate stage. The combination of these two initiatives, once implemented, dramatically changed roster management for coaches. Coaches now lose current athletes, while at the same time filling those gaps by recruiting from active players who have made themselves available. Talk about managing change. Team cohesion initiatives must now take this culture shift into account. I'm still asked if I miss coaching—I don't mind missing this part.

A few final thoughts about managing change with personnel. Veteran team members retire. Some are so indispensable that we actually do need two people to replace them. Others leave because of unrest, unresolved conflict or because you need them to. We may not be surprised when someone with a growing family looks to re-locate closer to supportive relatives. We will however, be very disappointed when a new arrival, stays long enough for a cup of coffee, then puts in their notice. Obviously, our emotional response will vary based on each circumstance.

Change also occurs when a key member of the team, perhaps with long tenure, chooses to depart for a new opportunity. We should not be surprised to lose someone who has been valuable, productive, and full of promise. The first part of managing this change is in our attitude about and for this person. What do you want your response to be to highly valued team members who are simply pursuing upward mobility? Especially, if they are finding opportunities elsewhere that you can't provide for them. Too often, I believe, leaders forget about our own career moves. Dad used to say, "You'll learn a lot about the people you work for, when you decide to leave".

When top quality team members inform us they are in a job search, this may also be the time that we fight to keep them. Should we lose that battle, and the change is imminent—what reaction is in the best interest of all involved? A first-class response would be to offer congratulations, and thank them for their service. Working closely with them in their final weeks of transitioning out of the job, might make things easier for their eventual replacement. Additionally, if we think long term—networking opportunities might lie ahead when a positive relationship is maintained. How someone exits our team, is just as important as how they enter.

EVALUATING CHANGE

When all is said and done, many leaders see managing the change as the last step, when in fact, we still need to evaluate the effectiveness. This is often overlooked, as it is only natural to keep our focus on the present. It won't take too many years of leading before you find yourself in a think tank with some employees or team members. The discussion will center on a change that is being proposed. One of the veterans in the crowd, might raise a hand and say, "Oh, you mean we need to change it back to the way we used to do it?"

Maybe we had it right in some instances. One of my favorite restaurants growing up was a real family business. They were always crowded, the food was amazing, and the location was a converted home. Along the way, they were able to expand to another part of the community in a more spacious and modern facility. Some years later, they moved back to the little homey spot they had occupied for so long. Clearly, they were able to evaluate the success associated with the move, and determined that they were better off before.

We can get stubborn as leaders when it comes to this type of thing. A well-defined process of change will include not only that the change will be evaluated over a period of time, but how that will be accomplished. What metrics, data, or results will be useful to determine if the change was for the better? Are we sure we will be able to obtain that information? Have we predetermined the time intervals for assessment? Let me be clear—I didn't spend any time forming questions like those early in my career. That is why I am sharing them here.

As we evaluate, we might also be feeling the impact of the change. I've developed the next scale with boating in mind. Weather changes can be swift and sudden. One of our first retirement bucket lists involved joining a boat club in the sunshine state. The administrators provide weather warnings, and updates daily. On some days, they prohibit the use of scheduled boats due to the forecast, and rightly so. In addition to giving wide berth to all rental boats, we have also learned to pay careful attention to scheduled tides, shifting winds, and threatening skies. On just a few occasions, we headed back a little too late to avoid pop up showers. Suddenly, everyone on board needed to huddle tightly under the Bimini to avoid getting soaked. When the wind pushes the rain in sideways, it's fairly miserable, and another lesson learned.

Perhaps the scale below, will help you evaluate the impact of an upcoming change you are leading.

## Impact of Change Scale

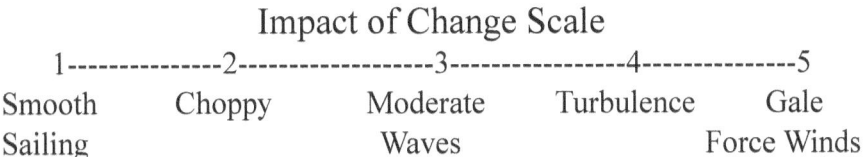

1---------------2--------------------3-----------------4---------------5
Smooth      Choppy      Moderate      Turbulence      Gale
Sailing                 Waves                      Force Winds

As you evaluate the effectiveness of a change, and the impact on those involved and effected—what will the huddle-up moment look like for your leadership team? You may need to withstand some turbulence, even major pushback. I guess the question to ask will be, "Is this the end we had in mind?"

Change occurs in so many different ways. We already reviewed the trust process back in Chapter Two, and much of that relates to change. Decision-making will be a central topic in Chapter Ten, and some of what is shared there will also overlap. A common denominator among each of these topics is the impact on people. As leaders in positions of authority, we have the responsibility to communicate that change is under consideration. We may outline a process intended to guide that change. Subordinates typically share in the process based primarily on the willingness of those leading to include them. As the leader, you will be making that decision.

Our focus remains connected to things ABOVE. In a competitive environment, we want to rise to the top, and often that means something has to change. Lofty goals and objectives occupy the thinking of highly motivated leaders. Hopefully, as you learn to lead through all the steps of change we have considered, you will gain confidence in yourself. Where did you first discover enough self-confidence to take on leadership? How are you instilling confidence in others? Our next chapter begins right there with a story you don't want to miss.

# Chapter Eight Review

- Effective leaders take the time to determine whether recent successes are effective indicators for what is to come.
- Plan the work → work the plan.
- The impactful leader will need to identify with the change.
- Make note of lessons learned in the past, seek out mentors for how best to lead change, and then step up and lead.
- Talent acquisition goes hand in hand with talent development.
- Take care of your people.

1 – How you look at change and any intermediate steps is what matters. Would you change the sequence below?

Anticipating Change

Planning Change

Challenging Change

Leading Change

Implementing Change

Managing Change

Evaluating Change

2 – When an important decision looms where change is needed, what approaches have you used or seen others used in healthy discussions to "challenge" team member's thinking about change?

3 – Cliches about change are interesting, "The more things change, the more they stay the same", "a change of heart", "you changed your tune", "change is inevitable, growth is optional". Circle one of the above and reflect on how it can be useful. Then, insert your own short list of phrases including "change" that come to mind, or have guided you at some point.

# Chapter 9 – That's "Your" Shot

The coach was guiding his basketball team (seeded #2) through the season-ending tournament, and as expected now faced the top team in the finals. His eight-year-old son was a "gym rat", and happily served as a manager, if only for the opportunity before and after every practice to shoot around on a real basketball court. The son was already determined to become a coach, and apart from just one practice, where he was too sick to attend, he didn't miss one. He studied and knew every play, every defense, and loved the car rides to and from practices and games, talking shop with the coach. One of the principles mentioned many times was the importance of preparation, and, "Not attempting to have a team try something in a game, they had not worked on in practice."

So, you can imagine the son's surprise, with only seconds remaining in the tied championship contest, when during a final time-out, this revered coach started outlining a play that was not in the playbook. The play was to end with one of the very solid players, but not one of the top scorers, getting the ball. The coach spoke with confidence, and informed the team that the opponent would anticipate one of two other players getting the ball at the end. He looked at the player designed to get the ball at his favorite spot on the court, and smiled when he completed the chalkboard session with a simple and precise statement to this player, "That's your shot".

His son was shocked, and could not understand why his father was breaking his own rule by charting out this last second play, that the team had never practiced. It wasn't the son's place to speak up....but as the team went out on the floor, he tried to get his father's attention, "But, Dad..." The coach looked his son in the eye, and said, "It will be ok". The son could only watch as the play began to evolve. The team had to go the full length of the court, and for the son, it all seemed to be in slow motion. He watched the diagram come to life, and right away he could see how loosely they were guarding the player who was going to take the shot. When he made his move from one side of the court to the left elbow of the free throw lane, he was wide open. He took the shot, and Swish! Game over.

As excited as the son was with the win, he was still deeply unsettled about what he had experienced. Eventually, when he was alone with his father, he said, "But Dad, you said never attempt something that you have not practiced, and we never practiced that play". A big smile came over the coach's face. He gave his son a pat on the shoulder, and said "Sure we did, we put that play in on the day you missed practice."

How do you instill confidence in others in your leadership role? The coach sent the designated shooter off with just the right words to keep in the back of his mind. The coach did not go to the result, which would have been a comment about making the shot. The coach certainly made the smart choice of not including any negative messages in the guidance. Athlete's must learn to manage the other voice in their head that says, "You're going to miss". This coach armed the shooter with something to help chase that negative thought away, "This is my shot."

The topic of confidence relates nicely to strengthening strengths, introduced in Chapter Six. In building relationships, whether as a parent with your kids or the boss at work, there is a great benefit to seeing and praising good work. When our kids exhibit good manners, thoughtfulness, and respectfulness or simply follow house rules, we don't want to miss the chance to reinforce that. As you observe your employees, colleagues, interns, or volunteers you have the chance to do the same thing. There is something to be said for immediate praise and feedback as it is observed. Compiling notes throughout the year of these observations will allow you to make them part of an annual evaluation and assessment. You will be able to fill the comment section with positive examples of how your team member responded or showed initiative in their behavior in a specific way.

Someone is always watching. Full disclosure—I was that "gym rat" manager, and I watched and listened carefully for all of that season. Even now, I reflect on the example he set. Dad must have observed how comfortable and successful, this certain player was when shooting from the left elbow of the free throw line. The last thoughts we give our players when they leave the huddle or dugout, or head off to the starting line for the mile run needs to instill confidence.

Dad told me plenty of stories of his earliest years of coaching, many occurred before I was born. One of my favorites involved a second-string JV basketball player. While he showed little promise at the time on the offensive end of the court, he had a great knack on defense to blanket whoever he was guarding. Surely, much to this JV player's surprise, he got called up late in the season, and was inserted in the varsity line-up with a big assignment. The opponent's top scorer had been unstoppable in an earlier meeting of the teams. The game plan came together, as the call-up started practicing with the varsity, and he heard the same message again and again, "Don't let him score, that's your job." The rest of the team would carry the offense, hiding their new starter who was designated primarily to set picks for his teammates. The stopper did his job that night. The opponent had no way of knowing about this defender, who over his career, developed into a top performer. Perhaps, change alone, was the victor in this scenario. Once a contest begins, the last thing you want in most cases, is for your opponent to feel comfortable. Taking their game plan away will clearly not always end up in a victory, especially if the opponent is simply better. This time, it worked!

How are you giving someone a chance? Do all team members know their role? Do you put yourself in a position to see what you need to see, in your organization? What does "developing someone" on your team look like? What are you looking for in recruitment of new employees? How about retainment? These are all good questions. Hopefully, instilling self-confidence into each of your team members is a key objective for you.

## Competence – Stages of Learning

How do you personalize a corporate training program? I spent some time with a specialist in this area a few years ago. There was one-on-one training, tutoring, and mentoring. It was all part of the process. Training and development may primarily be targeting efficiency and productivity. At the same time, on an individual basis, confidence arises out of increased competence.

As a leader, the competence of those working in your organization will show up. It will show up at the end of a production line, or in the quarterly sales report. Within our sports teams, most athletes recognize where they need to improve, and coaches will attempt to disguise their weaknesses.

A scouting report is intended to preview what to expect from an upcoming opponent. We also like to discuss with our team, what they will expect of us. Experienced coaches learn to scout themselves as well. My assistant coaches who offered related thoughts made a big impression on me. It may have been a simple statement that started with, "If I was coaching against us, I would ……" Coaching is teaching. That's not all that it is—but the ability to assess and enhance skill levels is foundational for a coach.

When teaching a sport skill, you need to recognize the stages of learning. The first stage is mental. You take on a youth basketball team, and introduce dribbling to the kids. Where should you start? Name the skill, describe its purpose, identify a few technical keys to success, provide a demonstration with those keys executed properly, and add in rules associated with that skill. Naturally, the next stage is practice.

Lots of practice will be needed. Initially, the dribbling might be attempted in a simple drill. Feedback is needed, but remember there are many types of feedback. Kids experimenting with dribbling might take one off the nose when they use too much power. They will struggle controlling the ball, and when you add movement, the errors will abound. As part of the practice stage, you would want to point out and keep reinforcing the keys to success, yet also begin to identify the common mistakes to avoid. Practice, practice, practice. Competence takes time.

At some point, the kids begin to compete and they put their developing dribbling skill to the test. The referee provides feedback, the ball will provide feedback, and the opponent stopping the dribble or stealing the ball will provide feedback. Self-confidence will be lacking in the early part of the practice stage, but as the skill develops, so too will the confidence.

Eventually, the day comes when that youngster with a couple of seasons under their belt, can dribble without thought, which means to some degree they have arrived at the automatic stage. Sure, more refinement is needed, and if we add a cross-over dribble to the mix, we go back to the practice stage. Former NBA star, Tim Hardaway Sr., is a great example of a cross-over dribble in the automatic stage. Dubbed the UTEP two-step, he not only mastered the technique, but also the confidence to use that at the highest level. His confidence was built right alongside each step of improvement.

Instilling confidence in those you are leading is a topic of great importance. As duties are assigned, especially those requiring new skills, you have to ask, is someone making sure that the keys to success are understood? Have common errors associated with these responsibilities been discussed? Do they get a chance to make errors? When an error is made, do they hear, "Good job", when in fact, it wasn't?

In training coaches over many years, this was a blind spot that I discovered in many developing coaches. What was meant by "good job" related to the effort in the attempt. Often, none of the technical keys being taught had been exhibited. Be aware that the learner will translate that feedback into thinking they performed correctly. A much better response when a good attitude attempt is full of errors would be to simply say, "Again". Have the learner repeat the attempt with consistent emphasis from you on the technical keys you are looking for.

Is 99.9% good enough? Not for air traffic controllers—we can agree on that. But in most careers, errors and mistakes will be part of the learning curve. Experience will be a great teacher, but as a leader you will need to determine and communicate to those you are leading, what mistakes are acceptable and which ones are not. Professional development, training sessions, shadowing, and direct supervision are all strategies that a leader needs to consider in terms of enhancing competence (performance) for those on your team.

Self-confidence is often linked to self-talk. This was illustrated in Chapter Three with the inner dialogue depicted with the ladder of success. Keep in mind, you will likely need to engage some individuals who show improvement, and begin to display over-confidence, perhaps even cockiness. This is especially concerning if there are any personal safety issues at risk. One other key aspect in helping someone gain competence is to regularly check for understanding. The Socratic method of asking questions is a great strategy to accomplish that for those learning, developing and growing in your organization.

## Commitment – Let's Start by Showing Up!

The restaurant serving staff double door highlights two significant terms (*in* and *out*) related to someone's commitment. Being seated a handful of times in well-established diners with doors like those in the illustration above, kept me on the edge of my seat whenever a wait staff headed for the wrong door. Clearly the doors are marked as a constant reminder of the flow needed to ensure that hot entrees piled on trays about to be delivered don't collide with empty plates and glasses being returned to the kitchen. *In* or *out* are two important descriptors to use in framing the topic of commitment.

### Team Commitment Scale

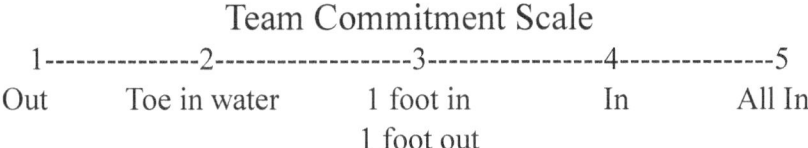

| 1 | 2 | 3 | 4 | 5 |
|---|---|---|---|---|
| Out | Toe in water | 1 foot in<br>1 foot out | In | All In |

From the perspective of team building, leaders need to know the commitment level of everyone in an organization. Any team member forcefully pulling in the opposite direction, simply not buying in, untrainable, and unproductive needs to be *out*. What are you waiting for? Have you addressed your concerns in a fair manner? Have you given a reasonable time period to see a favorable response? Then, in most cases, this person needs to be made available to other teams who may be seeking what they have to offer.

A caution in team settings for someone who appears to be *out* relates to when they may never have felt accepted, or worse, actually been excluded in some way. Not all teams welcome newcomers well. Have you addressed this in your culture? You may have checked the box of filling an open position, yet have no effective orientation program in place. One way to ensure that every new team member is welcomed, is to assign a mentor to them.

The other side of this scenario was one that I experienced often in pre-season. I would casually check in with our recruits— now on our roster—to see how the transition was going. All too often, they would gush about, "How great everything was". Of course, this made me proud of my returning players who were building on the foundation of previous teams who treated newcomers in the same positive way they had been welcomed. About mid-season when I checked back in, the same newcomer had found plenty of flaws and disappointments to comment on. Reality sets in. Tension, discouragement, and fatigue begin to play a role in the experience of any team member. Find ways to develop a culture of encouragement for the teams you are leading, and keep the lines of communication open early on for newcomers.

I also had a fair number of new players, who appeared to be just sticking their *toe in the water* to see if it was safe to go in. Reminds me of trips many years ago to Sand Beach in Bar Harbor, Maine in the early months of summer. You can count on a polar bear plunge almost any month of the year along the rocky coast of Maine. Newcomers to a team will often appear hesitant and in fairness, we should expect it to take some time for them to settle in. Our new players likely found the daily intensity level of their teammates to be a good bit higher than what they had experienced in high school or even at the club level.

Most new players needed twelve months to truly be ready and prepared for a collegiate season. They needed to experience the rigor of training and a highly competitive schedule at this new level. They also needed time to establish themselves in taking on the responsibilities that come with living away from home for the first time. As a team builder, all intentional work you do to welcome, train, and support new team members will pay dividends.

What are the repercussions for the organization when someone has *one foot in and one foot out?* Essentially they are out, but still in. This could be the leader or a follower. Perhaps, the leader has been looking for their dream job quite secretly for a year, yet guiding a company with significant responsibilities. If the Board of Directors, or whoever has the ultimate authority for the welfare of the future of the organization knew that, would they intercede? Not if they had a leader with integrity, who intends to do their very best, right up to their final day on the job. A different example could be the multi-year veteran, who makes no bones about their dissatisfaction with the team. In spite of that, they continue showing up and drawing a salary and compensation benefits, despite more often than not, pulling in their own direction. Interesting dynamics to consider.

## Commitment is observable.

Team members who are *in* are easy to spot. Those who will follow and be influenced by you, will determine for themselves how committed you are to your work, to them, and to practicing what you preach. A commitment to improve, achieve or excel impacts our confidence in a good way. Not believing in ourselves can be a permanent barrier, unless somehow we break through the doubt, negative self-talk, or fear of failure. A self-fulfilling prophecy really does work both ways.

I don't know about you, but the *Rudy* type of movie or story creates such a positive feeling inside. Despite the odds, Daniel "Rudy" Ruettiger—gets on the field. Notre Dame Football Coach, Ara Parseghian, delivers a memorable line to one of Rudy's teammates who had not reached his potential. That player is told, "If you had a tenth of the heart of Reuttiger, you'd have made All American by now!"[15] As leaders, we need to model our commitment level with our heart, our head, and our hands.

Team members who are *all-in*, who show commitment daily and do all they can for the cause, however you define that, will gain your confidence. Find those people. Early in my career, in recommending someone very highly, there was a timing issue on when this person could begin the job. I knew the hiring supervisor, and that person knew me. I made an extra call as the offer came in, and the potential new hire needed just a few months to complete a degree and related duties he had committed to. In that call, all I said to his future boss was, "This person is worth waiting for". The seasoned leader did in fact wait to bring his new employee on board, and it certainly ended up being a win-win.

Don't be in such a rush to climb in your profession, that you take your eye off the prize. The prize needs to be what you signed up for, accepted, and agreed to do. Show commitment to that work daily. Add value. When the day comes that you need to let your supervisor know you have started to look at a potential career move, that approach will pay off. I heard some good advice on this topic from an emerging leader I have been mentoring for some time. She said, "The best approach to advancing your career, is to be the best at your current role. Make an impact there, and always be where your feet are." One additional thought—don't forget to pass that forward when you get behind the *big desk*. Don't be the leader who benefited from a handful of opportunities, advancements, and promotions and then not be part of helping others advance in their careers. Lead others in a way that represents how you would want to be guided, supervised, developed, and supported.

Be an independent thinker. Be creative in your problem solving. Develop your own leadership scales to help you consider lots of options, and listen carefully to opposing views. At the end of the day, make high integrity choices with the values that align with your mission statement, and armed with all the lessons learned from the rear-view mirror. So, we've looked BELOW, BEHIND, and ABOVE. Come along, we have one last stop AHEAD in the *A²B² Leadership* framework.

## Chapter Nine Review

- Instilling confidence in your team members needs to be a key objective for a leader.
- Self-confidence in our competencies is often linked to our self-talk.
- Commitment is observable.
- Show commitment to your responsibilities daily.

1 – Remind yourself below of someone who showed confidence in you. Who gave you "your shot"?

2 – How can the stages of learning (mental, practice, automatic) be helpful as you train and develop your team members?

3 – Competence precedes confidence. Thoughts?

4 – Where did you fall on the commitment scale. Which of your team members is the most all-in? Perhaps reward that today in some way.

5 – What re-framing needs your attention right now?

# AHEAD →

"Take dead aim" is commonly attributed to golf guru, Harvey Pennick, and serves as sage advice for a golfer each time the tee is placed in the ground. This concept can easily apply to leaders looking to chart a course. Casting a vision seems to come so naturally to some, who appear unafraid to confront any fear of failure. Many visionaries not only see a future (AHEAD), but can envision the steps to success in chasing a dream. That pursuit will be enhanced when you can confidently rely on your Integrity Switch to light the way.

Most often, the end lies AHEAD. A vacation, a career, even a mortgage all have a start day and a finish day. An athletic season, a foliage season in New England, or a season of life loom AHEAD, eventually commence—and at some point, will draw to a close.

The more actionable phrase "moving ahead" may resonate more strongly for you and provide applicable insight in the arena where you lead. As you move into these final chapters, remember that *beginning with the end in mind* has been a backdrop right from the outset, and perhaps no better spot in this book to apply that than in our next chapter.

# Chapter 10 – GAP Leadership

My brother Dan, among other things, is an artist. I could never color inside the lines, and had no interest in improving in that area. My creativity is in writing, or preparing to deliver a presentation or motivational speech. Allow me, however, to paint a picture in your mind to introduce what I like to refer to as Gap Leadership.

"You are the soccer goalie, with the score nil to nil and the clock is ticking in the final overtime period….12…11….10. Just then, an opposing striker surprisingly dodges between your fullback and sweeper who collide and tumble to the ground. With several full speed strides, the striker is now completely clear of any defender—but you. You are in the gap! "What are you playing for, goalie?" This is the pressing question that I hope will create some great discussion when I use this scenario in a seminar setting.

After allowing time for participants to think, I will re-start the clock....9....8....7, then ask, "What tactics or techniques might you employ?"

Some common participant comments have included:

- If the goalie is going to make a move it better happen sooner than later.
- The goalie should use a "surprise" all-out attack and charge the attacker.
- The goalie should cut down the angle, taking away the high percentage shot.

Usually in a group setting, I will ask for a volunteer to take on the role of the goalie, and stand in front of the group holding a sign with GAP printed in very large letters. I start the clock once more, 6....5....4, then ask the goalie, "What are you playing for?" I ramp up the pressure—with rapid questioning—as the clock keeps ticking....3...."The result is in your hands, what are you playing for?" ...2..."It's all up to you, what are you playing for?" Usually by now, the goalie has offered a few responses, so I would turn to the rest of the participants, and invite their input.

Often, I need to refer participants back to the essential question, "But what is the goalie playing for?" Eventually, I might get a comment like, "To preserve a tie, because anything short of that will result in a defeat." Since a tie could lead to penalty shots—a correct response might be "To keep hope alive for a win".

What a tough spot for that goalie to be in. We can all agree with that, but what is the main objective of the activity? The purpose is to give everyone a feeling of standing in the gap. What was the last tough spot you were in? Were you able to define the "gap" you stood in? Was it an integrity gap? Were you faced with an ethical dilemma? Was it a gap representing handling a crisis or recovering from a failure? Is there a gap in a vision you have cast, and clear steps to close the gap? Remember Sharon in the time-out. She saw the close of the match coming and the scoreboard was not looking good. She literally stepped in the gap between what was happening and what needed to happen and found a way to inspire.

Like the goalie, sometimes we don't have time on our side to sit and think. In the vice grip of a most difficult "gap" you find yourself standing in, are you able to recognize what is at stake? How do you handle the pressure-cooker moments, when time is running out, and a decision must be made? Who do you lean on in gap situations? Is your integrity switch hard-wired by now? If so, you will be able to trust your instincts, even in the toughest times.

Gap Leadership is represented in my $\mathbf{A^2B^2}$ model under AHEAD. The clock is always ticking, which means we are in one sense or another always moving AHEAD. That does not mean we are getting AHEAD. Leaders stand in the gap regularly with due dates and deadlines needing attention. The same is true for your team members, with assignments coming from you. You can get a lot of mileage out of conversations with your team focused on this gap leadership concept. It is not surprisingly—applicable to other aspects of our lives as well.

Generally, there is no substitution for preparation—we discussed this earlier. Being out ahead of upcoming challenges and impending decisions often pays dividends with favorable outcomes. In Chapter Two (page 14), I shared the MBWA story of being in the gap over a period of time, with a deadline attached where I needed to make a decision. That particular decision, as is often the case, impacted a lot of people. As you step into leadership, you must prepare to step up and make some tough decisions.

# Decision-making

We don't always have the luxury of having time on our hands with challenges that confront us, certainly not in a crisis scenario. This is also true when as the leader, the "tyranny of the urgent" arrives in your doorway. This occurred, in my professor role, more than a handful of times with students looking for an extension for an assignment due that day. In many cases, after listening to a laundry list of excuses, I went with the oft-used, "A lack of planning on your part, does not constitute an emergency on mine". Parenting teens also comes to mind here. It's 6:30 pm on a Friday night, and all of sudden, you hear for the first time about a "wonderful" social opportunity for your teen that requires her to be on her way by 6:45. Previous discussions with agreed upon "rules of the road" help during those exchanges.

Carving out time to arrive at a decision is essential. Being in the right frame of mind to make decisions is also essential. What professional habits have you established in making decisions? The ability to focus on what is in front of us as leaders is clearly a step to success in decision-making. Consciously setting aside distractions, being able to compartmentalize an issue at hand, and giving it your full attention are all a part of developing leadership skills.

"How is that working out for you?", which I mentioned earlier, is commonly used to challenge someone on their decision-making. That prompt may prove helpful if we tend to repeat the same mistake. What emotional guardrails do you have in place, when serious life events require your attention at the same time that significant decisions at work are looming? When upon reflection we are not pleased with a decision we made, might we discover that not being in balance personally is a major contributor.

Perhaps outlining the types of decisions leadership will require of you is a good stepping off point for you. We have daily decisions—both personal and professional. On the personal side, do you place emphasis on Spirit, Mind and Body? This is ingrained in me from my long association with Springfield College—where each is emphasized philosophically as part of our educational mission, and represented as a side of our inverted triangle.

How do you activate your Spirit daily? Daily disciplines that engage your Spirit can bring great personal benefit. I enjoy opening my Bible, reading Scripture, and working through my prayer journal to start the day. This routine also gets my mind working, and I tend to be fairly productive in the early morning hours. Fitness comes next, and I always try to get my workouts in or make tee times before noon.

Depending on your inclination, you may have discovered that exercising the body comes first, which awakes the soul, then comes sound thinking. The Greek adage "a sound mind in a sound body" illustrates that focusing on these personal elements may enhance your effectiveness. There will be days ahead as a leader that will feel like a long haul, so you must take care of yourself. Meeting the basic needs of nourishing yourself in spirit, mind, and body may be the key to avoiding decision-making failures.

Establish a routine that allows you to organize your thoughts before you rush headlong into the sea of daily tasks and decisions that await you as a leader. When working within a leadership team, I have observed that leaders are quick to identify challenges, and consider options to solve them. I also have noticed they are not always willing to plan the work needed for those solutions. The lost art of thoughtfulness is often a root cause for a failed decision or action.

Apply this to your last moment of remorse about a decision. Not being in a good place emotionally and psychologically early in your work day can be hazardous to your leadership. Our emotions may push recent procrastination aside, which is not necessarily a bad thing. Unless, you decide to plunge headlong into the number one contentious issue that needs a decision, and rush that process. When we are out of balance, we might choose not to include others who need to be part of decision-making conversations.

I recently asked a business owner about her thoughts on this topic. She responded, "Be intentional in decision making, and don't make big decisions without thinking through all potential outcomes". She added some questions to consider. "Does this decision support long and short-term goals? Could something go wrong if the decision is made? Is there an alternative decision that could be made?" She wrapped this up with, "Then sleep on it".

Our leadership style and philosophy have a lot to do with how decisions are made in our program or company. It's easy in an interview for a leadership candidate to share that they are ultra collaborative. Taking that position probably backfires, when what the chief executive is really looking for is someone decisive, who can quickly identify all possible options for an obstacle that has emerged. Effective collaboration will be built over time, and it means you will have the right people participating, who you can count on to provide helpful input based on their expertise.

Think of the NASA mission control room scenes in a movie. As the countdown begins for the takeoff; specialists begin signing off that they are a "Go". All of the synchronized functions and features need to be successfully confirmed in sequence for the launch to occur. The all-important decision to "go" for this high performing team is a result of meticulous planning, and expert insight when the pressure is on. Imagine how deeply those strapped in astronauts are *trusting the process* (a Chapter Two topic) in those final pre-launch decisions.

Some decisions require a collaborative effort, but others don't. The trick for leaders is to make that determination first, and then develop a method for communication and input to be received. The decisions you have been allowed to make, should give you a pretty good idea of the level of authority you have been entrusted with. We must keep in mind, just as trust has been placed on us to make decisions, we should also be providing decision-making opportunities for those we are supervising or leading.

I can still remember the first time I drove the family car alone. I had just completed driver education, passed my road test, and finally had my license in hand. My parents made that decision. While I didn't think about it at the time, the day came when I was part of making that decision for all three of our children. A lot goes through your mind as you watch *your* car back out of the driveway, and *speed away*!

Our women's volleyball team developed a method of collaborating and communicating that may have looked simple from the outside looking in. In reality, the idea of standing together in a circle to have real conversations actually took a number of years to develop. The process started simply enough, as the players were asked to take part in making a decision. Some ideas "take a life of their own", and that is the case with the following team activity.

This one season, I came upon the idea that perhaps our team cohesion and competitive grit could be improved. To accomplish this, I established a couple of weekly awards that represented those characteristics we were looking for. I bought a box of glue sticks, and went to the local big box construction supply store and purchased a box of 6-inch nails. After the first weekend of competition, I circled the team up at the very beginning of a Monday practice to review our tournament performance. The team was informed that they were going to select two award winners. The rules were presented as follows when I shared, "Once you hear the description of each award, you will be asked to point at one member of the team who deserves that award. You all need to continue pointing at that team member until I count the votes".

I then held up one of the nails for everyone to see, and said, "Ok team, that was a tough tournament with challenging competition we just completed. Who gets the nail for this week which represents our toughest competitor over the weekend?" Slowly, of course, fingers started to be displayed and this visual scoreboard emerged. I wondered if someone might point at themselves, since the rules did not prohibit that, but I don't recall that ever happening. Some peer influencing appeared as some players waited for the independent thinkers in the group to openly choose, and eventually everyone was pointing at someone. I did a quick count, congratulated the winner, handed her that big spike, then added some comments about the competitive spirit of this player that we had all witnessed.

Next up, was the glue stick, and I introduced it like this: "All right, one more award. I am looking for the player you all believe did the most to help us 'stick' together in that tournament. Now that you know the rules, go ahead and select." The glue stick presentation generally allowed for some nice comments on the positive attitude and selflessness of that player. We did that for a year, and as I observed the process and results, I began to see that in a way the foundation was forming for something I was searching for. I wanted to help the players talk openly, candidly, and accurately about our performances and progress.

The season of weekly team decisions was done as a positive award ceremony. This was memorable for our players. Years later, at an alumnae game, one of them brought her glue stick, and showed it to me. "This award meant a lot to me", she said. As the next season commenced, and on one of those early morning runs, I began to see a way to expand this activity. What I am about to share now, as I have many times in leadership or coaching clinics comes with a disclaimer. I don't think you should necessarily do this. The best ideas are often the ones we develop through trial and error. So, don't follow my lead here until and unless you have identified the purpose for your team. If you choose to attempt this, start slowly to build trust, until you believe the team is ready for a deeper conversation.

So, the next season, we start up the same activity but within a few weeks, as any coach would expect—flaws in attitude, effort, performance and focus naturally were exhibited. I also took note of how many players were not pointed at during the nail and glue voting. I hoped those individuals noticed this as well. To ensure they were aware, and to address some of our shortcomings, I took this activity very quickly to another level.

Once the players were all pointing, and the count had been taken, I asked a very powerful follow-up question, "Who is pointing at you?"

The circle was quiet, so I let that sink in, and said, "Seriously, take a good hard look, is anyone pointing at you?" I allowed for a good bit of silence, and eventually had them vote on the second award, and once again I said, "Who is pointing at you?" Out of this sort of rhetorical question, emerged what I had really been looking for all along. We started to see a bit more competitive fire in our practices, and more encouragement flowing among the players.

My final teams developed in part through this simple activity, the ability to have real, adult conversations with each other. Over time, I would enter that circle at the outset or end of a practice, and ask some pretty pressing questions. Often, I would start by asking, "Can we have an adult conversation"? My definition of that shared with the team was simply, an eye to eye, in-person dialogue together. As the leader, I got better at crafting some good, hard questions. These were moments where I learned to be comfortable with the silence, as I waited for the first response to eventually come from somebody.

I am not sure how you can apply this circling up part of our culture in your work space, but I wish I had come up with this many years prior. Here are some results of this simple activity that we initiated. First of all, the visible vote for one teammate for each award, communicated appreciation for and support to a teammate. As mentioned earlier, I began to see that I was facilitating a type of fierce conversation for sure. Each player was not just sending a message to the teammate receiving their vote, but also sending a message to all their teammates they were not pointing to.

How do you help others develop decision making skills? I bumped into a good example having lunch with my oldest son and a close friend of his. I asked them what lesson from a leader they had learned on the job. My son talked about a supervisor who made a lasting impression on him by how he developed decision-making skills in others. When a serious issue arose, the supervisor would gather all those on the shift who reported to him, and asked them, "How would you handle this?" This leader employed guided discovery as a teaching method—with all involved in the discussion. When a solution that would likely go poorly was suggested, the supervisor would facilitate a discussion. These conversations were designed to allow team members to recognize on their own how a suggested response could be faulty, and learn without making that error. This supervisor's approach fits very well with the historic piece of advice, "Tell me and I'll forget, teach me and I may remember, involve me and I learn."

Here is a challenging thought about your leadership. Think about this conversation that was occurring years after my son had made some career moves, where that leader was being discussed in a very positive fashion because of his impact. Years from now, what will your followers be saying about you?

## Leaders must be prepared to make tough decisions.

Speaking of career moves—a new leadership opportunity came my way soon after—what ended up to be my final season of coaching. Right up to the last match where our team was battling in an NCAA regional championship, I did not know that would be my final day on the sidelines. What a great way to go out, with such a special group of people. In retrospect, how neat to end my coaching career, working with a team completely focused on a championship run, and not distracted by an impending coaching change. But. . . talk about a tough decision. Any time you work with people, these decisions are a challenge, but forty collegiate seasons was enough. Plus, Dad always said, "Get out of coaching before *they* want you to."

Many of those women on my final team are coaching today, or achieving careers in their fields. Lucky for me, the physical therapists in that group, answer their phones when I call to describe my most recent back, hip, or shoulder ailment preventing me from golfing. They send me photos of stretches, and it allows me to stay connected. I admire this group greatly, and while the connection with some may be my simple "Happy B'Day!" Facebook greeting; I remember each of them fondly. A neat bond with others can develop from opportunities with this thing called leadership. Don't miss that.

# Continuous Improvement

I mentioned Marcus Jannitto earlier in my story about Bonusball (page 44). Our collaboration has continued throughout the years. Marcus led leadership training sessions at my long running volleyball camp, and we have co-presented together in leadership seminar sessions. He was a frequent guest speaker during my long tenure as a professor. I always felt that I learned as much as my students during these visits. This was the case when he was invited to share some leadership perspectives in the coaching principles class I was teaching in the 1990's. As I recall, the lesson title was Total Quality Athletics. It had such a positive impact on our students and with his permission, I used his outline for many years to come. This was the first time I heard about TQM (total quality management).

Marcus adapted two key concepts of *continuous improvement* and *customer satisfaction*, and applied them for leadership in coaching. Of course, our guest speaker had many years serving in the RI Air National Guard as a navigator, so he had experienced the benefits as it related to the emphasis on continuous improvement. I can't think of a better topic to wrap up this chapter than with the idea of looking AHEAD optimistically for ways to improve.

In 37 years of running a summer volleyball camp, I believe that right from the start, every closing awards ceremony highlighted Most Improved as the top award. The number one objective for every camper was to help them improve in the short time we had together. How do you place value on continuous improvement in your organization? Do the annual performance audits recognize specific areas of improvement? Do individuals gain recognition for those improvements? What are the metrics you use not only to assess results, sales, production, or the financial bottom line, but also improvements on how you do things? Remember back in Chapter Three (page 22), the illustration of the ladder of success?

How can a leadership scale help us see where we are in the gap between "I won't" and "I will"?

## Success Scale

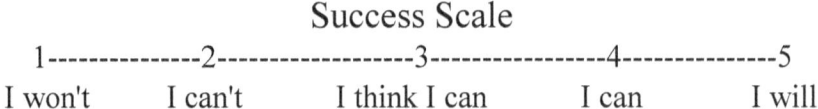

You will have the chance in the chapter review, to develop / modify this scale on your own. In guiding and encouraging others, how can this scale be helpful to those who believe they can't? "I might", "I'll try", and "I'll strive" are other descriptors, not included in this scale. You might find those options to be more meaningful than those I selected. By the way, what is the difference between trying and striving? That is a topic worth exploring.

Marcus introduced the topic of customer satisfaction by asking students to consider both internal and external customers and relationships in athletics. I found it most useful at the time in my own coaching to identify my customers, and attempt to determine my impact on them. Hopefully, your wheels are turning as you think about the current state of affairs of your leadership role, or the responsibilities you have taken on under the guidance of a leader. You may see some things that your leader does not. Be ready the next time you are asked for input, on how things could be improved.

I'm not quite done with some related thoughts on continuous improvement. I will pick it back up in Chapter Twelve with comments on goal setting. I'll be using a Latin phrase in connection with a powerful and historic athletic connection to do just that. Hopefully, that piques your interest, but first we need to shift to the topic of adversity.

## Chapter Ten Review

- In the vice grip of a most difficult gap you find your-self standing in, are you able to recognize what is at stake?
- Leaders must be prepared to make tough decisions.
- Years from now, what will your followers be saying about you?
- Two major tenants of TQM: continuous improvement and customer satisfaction.

1 – Have you felt a leadership pinch of being in the gap with a decision you must make that will impact others?

Describe a GAP you find yourself in right now.

2 – How can you enhance your daily routine in Spirit, Mind, and Body?

3 – Have you disagreed in the past with a decision made by a leader, but later on, you gained a different perspective on that decision?

4 – What are your thoughts on continuous improvement as part of Total Quality Management?

Follow up: To what degree are you satisfying your customers? Do you know, and if so, how do you know?

5 – What does moving from "I won't" or "I can't" look like for you? Design your own leadership scale.

### YOUR Success Scale

1---------------2-------------------3-----------------4--------------5

_____        _____        _____        _____        _____


OPTIONS: I can        I think I can        I'll fail
         I can't        I tried        I'll strive
         I did        I will        Other:
         I might        I won't

# Chapter 11 – Overcoming Adversity

L et's go back to late 1999, and the excitement and anxiety regarding Y2K. Almost everyone had an eye out for the year 2000 when the traditional Times Square countdown on New Year's Eve, would celebrate the new millennium. I remember anticipating how strange it was going to feel to write the year on a bank check starting with 20, rather than 19. Behind the scenes, plenty had been done, and needed to be done with computer coding to move from two digits to four digits.

I am far from qualified to do justice in a discussion related to the world's response to preparing for Y2K adversity, mainly with technology. In anticipation of calamity if everything relying on a computer malfunctioned, Y2K survival options began to emerge. In our family, the emergency preparedness plan eventually was settled on with a budget maximum of $20. We loaded up with plenty of gallon jugs of water, enough batteries to keep our flashlight going for the winter, and what surely resulted in a ten-year supply of matches. The January, 1999 front cover of TIME magazine included "The End of the World?"[16] Billions were spent to prepare for potential disaster that never came.

Most of us are quite practical and realistic in establishing contingency funds for unforeseen emergencies. The transmission goes on our car, or the roof leaks the month after our 20-year warranty expires. We need some funds set aside. This takes discipline, and a willingness to look AHEAD and be prepared.

> If adversity is defined as, "Difficulties or misfortune",
> then leadership provides a generous helping.

Group dynamics in the best of circumstances creates many challenges. As each season progresses, most coaches value and encourage an attitude of mutual appreciation among teammates. How do we look or scan AHEAD in the people business we have chosen as a career? What will be the early signs of adversity among your troops? Think about the level of cohesion you believe your team has developed. Notice I said "think" about the level they have developed. Have you given this some thought?

Much of our in-season workload as coaches is given to organizational and administrative duties, travel arrangements, and quick turnarounds from one match or tournament to another. Add in recruiting duties, along with a never-ending list of things to work on in the next practice, and your plate is full. Thus, the ever-present struggle with work/life balance. The point is this—with all that going on (or whatever your weekly regimen looks like), are you aware of tension that is developing or already exists among your team members? If, at the heart of all we do daily in coaching, is intended to be in the best interests of our student-athletes, then we must pay attention to the dynamics developing within the group.

Let's start with internal competition. To the degree that you have a lot of talent on your team, your players are pushing every day to either stay in your line-up or get in your line-up. Some of your players will experience inner turmoil about the role that has been given to them. This can easily cause friction between teammates.

Secondly, a coach makes how many hundreds of decisions each season? What are the chances that some of those won't create dissension in the ranks, or be perceived in some cases as inconsistent? I was never happy with all my decisions, so why would I expect others to be? A fair bit of tension accompanies the coach/player relationship, and the same will be true in a business setting where co-workers are vying for the advancement opportunity that was just announced.

Hopefully, as leaders, our philosophy holds firm, the expectations that we have in place are adhered to, and a positive team culture becomes reality. Despite your best efforts as a coach, you experience a player quitting, a dispute erupts between teammates, or you "hear" that one or more of your players is not "buying into" your leadership. Strive as we might to develop outstanding cohesion, it only takes one disgruntled player to dismantle a lot of what you have been trying to build.

Setbacks to team building efforts will occur. How can you best prepare to handle those? Knowledge is power. Some active listening is helpful. Going back to Chapter Three (page 26), relationship building requires real conversations. Reasoning with individuals who you suspect are disrespectful or instigating problems needs to occur. Scheduling a conversation is a nice way to stem a potential conflict.

Once the meeting is confirmed, prepare a few open-ended questions. Maybe start with, "How are *you* doing?" Allow what you hear to do the heavy lifting early in the conversation. At some point, you might want to say, "How are *we* doing?" This may help move the conversation to a place where your team member begins to name their objections with you. These *concerns* may include your approach, your style, or your decisions that have impacted them.

One pro-active approach I used was to have a brief side conversation during practice. I would look for a time when players were rotating in and out of tactical activities, or perhaps during cool-down at the very end of our training session. I might also invite a player to get to practice a little early for some extra work with a particular skill, and take a few minutes during that time to engage in conversation. Often, after a few minutes of dialogue, it would make sense for me to suggest that we schedule some time together to discuss further, "topics" that had emerged.

In some circumstances, detecting an issue within a team sadly comes too late. Behind the scenes, the leader is often the last to know about a squabble among team members. I was not always quick on the uptake in sensing signs of dis-unity but over time I learned to recognize a few. Take note when your internal radar is shouting that "something" is wrong. It may be a practice with subpar energy or experiencing an unexpected or disastrous match performance that gets your attention. When I got to the point that I wanted to ask the group, "Where is my team and what did you do with them?", it was obvious that our team needed some cohesion repair attention.

A lesson I learned the hard way is the importance as the leader to consider a picture frame when attempting to identify team cohesion issues. In a seminar setting, I like to hold up an empty picture frame as part of introducing this concept, while asking, "Does this frame represent a mirror or a window?" Allowing for some silence, and perhaps moving around the available space and among the participants, I might add, "When you recognize an issue with your team, are you more likely to look first at yourself as the culprit or others as the cause?" The frame in your hand can represent a mirror, and serve as a reminder to do some self-assessment. Once that is done, that same frame can represent a window with your team in full view—where you suspect the problem is originating."

"Considering the mirror" relates to the earlier discussion in Chapter Four on blind spots. Disconnects develop between team members and leaders all the time. If how you lead, or simply how you handle or avoid handling a problem has a negative effect within your circle of influence, you may be the last to know. If you determine that you aren't the primary source of turmoil, then it's time to look *through that picture frame* at those who may be the cause. So then, what do you do? As a coach, you might scrap the practice plan, put the balls away, and circle up the chairs for "a team meeting". The leader who takes the time to dig below surface communication will likely begin to recognize issues that need attention.

Truthfully, sometimes it has to get worse before it gets better. Do your best in this gathering to facilitate the conversation. Often when some of the "baggage" gets put out there in front of everyone, that is enough. Sometimes venting, and feeling safe doing that, is all that is needed. When a conflict between teammates is discovered, you may want to facilitate a discussion, and start with some ground rules. Establishing boundaries for healthy dialogue will help to avoid additional or collateral damage. You might discover, that within a day or two, those involved decide to meet and talk things over, or team leaders might arrange a players-only session.

There are two things I learned related to these types of situations. Whatever the cause of strife or internal conflict is, until it *gets named* in front of everyone, it is not likely to be fixed. Secondly, however you circle your team up, one thing *is* certain—all the problems are in that circle. More importantly, so are all the solutions. Hopefully for my teams, the volleyballs came back out of the baskets sooner than later. Very often, some renewed appreciation for the opportunities in front of the team outweighed nagging issues.

As we continue to explore the topic of adversity, be thinking about the levels of adversity you have faced as a leader. Was your integrity challenged in some way? We encounter setbacks, sustained opposition, and damaging incidents in leadership roles. You will need conviction of purpose, diligence, and perseverance to withstand the storms that are coming your way. Remember as long as you pay attention, you will gain wisdom and discernment from each tough situation you handle. The hope is that eventually, we can view adversity episodes in the rearview mirror, and move AHEAD. Let's move now from preparing for and handling adversity to the reality of unexpected challenges.

## Washing Bananas - Who Would Ever Have Thought . . .

Some phrases, just seem to fit certain situations. Here's one, "Who would *ever* have thought…" This phrase may be the lead in for a conversation in regard to an incident, an accident, or perhaps a very surprising circumstance. That question might also apply when some-one's achievement and notoriety was at one time quite unlikely. Much has been made of Tom Brady's physical testing results with regard to athletic attributes, which despite quite a nice career at Michigan, made him a 6th round pick in his NFL Draft. Who would *ever* have thought Tom Brady would become arguably the GOAT—greatest of all time!

Have you *ever* seen something so unusual that it took time for your brain to register? On June 1, 2011, I stepped out of a store in western Massachusetts, just three miles from my house. I saw a wide black band in the sky with a triangle shape dangling from it. This was unlike any sky I had ever seen. It took a few moments, but instinctively I called home to my family and said, "Get downstairs, a tornado is coming right at you". This unexpected EF-3 tornado with wind gusts of 160 mph narrowly avoided our home but not our street, and left a 38-mile swath of damage to land in western Massachusetts. "Who would *ever* have thought….?"

Fast forward….April 2020…taking advantage of the early senior citizen covid hours to get some groceries. I was in and out quickly, and soon I was home with disinfectant wipes ready to clean items alongside Diane. While wiping down packages of paper towels and bags of frozen blueberries, I noticed that she had been busy at the sink. I stopped in my tracks when I saw a bunch of bananas in a bowl filled with soapy water. After quietly staring for several minutes, I snapped a photo of something I almost couldn't put into words. I thought to myself, "Wow—we are now washing bananas!"

Unexpected challenges await you in your leadership. Count on it. Sometimes a sport season felt like a runaway freight train. Sure, you tend to fall into a routine, but there was something about getting to the last few weeks of the regular season that made me question just how prepared our team was for the stretch run. I think that it was about this time each season when I started to talk with my staff and players about "expecting the unexpected".

Situational leadership comes to mind with that phrase. Coaching experience teaches you to prepare to help your team respond to the unexpected. Injuries are part of competitive sports, and provide an interesting example to consider. A fairly common occurrence is walking into a gym and seeing one of the top players on the opposing team in street clothes and using crutches. You know exactly how your mind works in those first few moments. First, I would hope that there is at least a twinge of feeling bad for any player going through that. Next, there is a fleeting moment of elation, when you think you have gained an advantage. After all, now you don't have to worry about this significant opponent. Then, because this is not your first rodeo, you recall similar circumstances in the past. A strong concern immediately presses in knowing that many on your team think they just gained points on the scoreboard without earning them.

Realistically, once you coach a few seasons, you have been on the other side of that equation in dealing with your team injuries. You will learn to recognize that every time someone goes down in your lineup, it provides a great opportunity for someone waiting in the wings. Often, a team really steps up in these situations. Going back to the example provided, generally I would gather the team right on the spot. I would acknowledge that it appears our preparation for this match just took an unexpected turn. Then, I would quickly remind them of a specific time we lost a key player, and made adjustments to overcome that. I can almost hear myself now saying something like, "Let's keep our focus right where it needs to be tonight, on each next point available."

Mental toughness is constantly tested in competitive environments. Creating a practice environment where you insert difficult challenges will help build resiliency. We made sure our players had ample opportunities to overcome adversity in our training sessions, because we knew what was AHEAD. They would trail on the scoreboard, and need to come back. They would at times lead handily in some sets, see momentum turn in favor of the opposition, and learn how to get back on track. These natural aspects of competition will relate to the competitive environments you are leading, and the challenges you place in front of your team members will give you a chance to see how they handle themselves.

A final thought on confronting unexpected challenges. Pay attention to how you handle stress and strain. The ability to *stay in the present*, is a challenge when something big blows up in front of you. Develop the ability to not allow one part of your day to effect the rest of it. Those we are leading look to us in times of trouble, especially unforeseen circumstances that could have negative consequences. Remaining calm, cool, and collected sure sounds good, but it's not always that easy. Place a reasonable amount of time and effort on challenging issues. When you do turn your attention to other business at hand—be fully present in each part of your day.

When you get a chance, spend time reflecting on the outcome of challenges you have faced. What standards are in place, or what constant review systems do you have to alert you, and thus avoid unexpected issues and challenges? I think as leaders, the more challenges we face, the more we learn to be pro-active.

In addition to unpacking failure, as discussed in Chapter Four, we can't overcome adversity without responding to it. One business leader I have spoken with, kept it simple. "Expect to be a professional problem solver. Listen. Reflect. Respond". Back in Chapter Five, we acknowledged that some extreme scenarios will rise to the level of a crisis. What are some of the lesson's history teaches us about crisis management? One that I paid attention to, is the fact that at times—how the crisis was handled, becomes more of the story than the crisis itself.

When problem solving, effective leaders pull out all the stops, right from the start at gathering information as quickly and efficiently as possible and from all parties concerned. There are situations that require some immediate action as well, but in many cases, a big mistake can be made at this point. If all the information has not been gathered and explored, this may not be the time for a decisive and final action to be taken. For example, highly volatile personnel situations, can be handled in stages. Give that strong consideration.

Unexpected setbacks offer you and your organization the opportunity to flex your adaptation muscles. Effective leaders adapt, and are able to avoid repeating the same mistakes. Effective leaders ensure that team members learn lessons from the tough spots that emerge. Don't neglect the need to make systematic changes if needed, to avoid repeated mistakes. As best you can, expect the unexpected.

## Motivation – Sources of Inspiration

Failure doesn't have to be final. In fact, responding to adversity and recovering from those circumstances, can provide great motivation to leaders. Whether we fall down, or get knocked down—we need to get back up, dust ourselves off, and move AHEAD. Our last chapter ended with the topic of continuous improvement—allow that to be your mindset and motivator to recover from adversity.

Motivating and inspiring others often seems mystical. One day our approach seems to work, but on the very next day—we get it all wrong. I often greeted coaches attending my clinics over the years, with an offer and an index card. "Please write down the pressing question you came here with today", was the offer I would give. At the close or opening of a session, I would pull out a card, read it to the group and briefly address it. If I had kept a running log of the questions submitted, I am confident that, "How do I motivate my players?" would be in the top three. My stock response has been, "How often do you use a scoreboard in practice"? The phrase "competitive cauldron" was popularized by

Women's Soccer Coach, Anson Dorrance, when he was coaching the likes of Mia Hamm at the University of North Carolina. The essence of this approach, when taken to its extreme in practice, is that everything is scored. If we want to impact the motivational levels of our players, then make sure they are competing for something on a regular basis.

Coaches need to gauge the motivational level of our players, and with experience learn when, and how frequently to use a pep talk. We may feel obligated prior to every contest to shout something like, "Win just one for the Gipper" to get our group busting down the locker room door. If that phrase is new to you, it will be worth your time to look up the history that relates to Notre Dame football coach Knute Rockne, and how he used this "dying wish" of halfback, George Gipp in a pep talk. Keep in mind, not all athletes need a pep talk, nor will they all respond the same to your exhortations. Coaches might mistakenly believe they are duty-bound to deliver pep talks all the time. You are creating that gap, and that expectation of yourself—perhaps because that is all you know. That may have been how you were coached.

Have I mentioned, "Less is more" at all? This might be a good time to consider that principle. I do believe that every leader will need to activate some motivational skills. Personally, I never believed that I had the secret to motivating players, but I did experiment with different approaches—both with individuals and the team. More than anything, I wanted players to compete with confidence, and I tried to press buttons or create scenarios that might feel powerful to them. I remember often asking one of my setters right before game time, "Are you ready?" My confidence was always boosted when the same reply was always given, "Coach—I was born ready!"

"Timing is everything", and not just related to comedians and their punch lines. One of my favorite pep talks, emerged over the course of a season for one of my men's teams. The back story goes something like this. Without the team knowing it, all season long as a weekly voter on the national poll—I was using my first-place vote on our team, since we were unbeaten in our division. There was also another unbeaten team, ranked 1st all year, who received the majority of first place votes weekly. We were on a collision course to see them at championship time. Every week, I made a big deal of our #2 ranking, especially the fact that we never had more than one first-place vote. Of course, the hope was that this would keep them hungry and eager for each match. I reminded them constantly that apparently, they had a lot to prove.

Sure enough, that particular squad is sitting in a meeting room hundreds of miles away from our home court, preparing for the long-awaited showdown between the nation's top two undefeated teams. Now, it's not like my team needed motivation—they were a highly motivated group. It was however, a very interesting match-up. These two highly successful teams were built quite differently. Simply put, our success on the court would be determined by great ball control, and a fast tempo on offense. We needed to play our game, and trust all the parts. They out-sized us considerably, and were a powerful team, but not nearly as quick as our guys. With that in mind, it was time to pull out all the aces I had been holding.

We gathered around for our routine pre-match scouting report, and mixed in a few points of emphasis in terms of the tactics we favored in this match-up. Then, I pulled out a folder, and said "Oh by the way, I guess I never mentioned to you that I was one of the national poll voters this season. I thought you might like to see a copy of my votes". So, around the room went the copies of my weekly votes and of course, they discovered where their "one single" first-place vote came from— each and every week.

I would not attribute the 3-0 win that day to a motivational ploy— not at all. I had a team full of future college coaches on that squad (no less than five of that group have coached at that level), and we had a lot going for us. On the other hand, there is something to be said for "timing", and I had hoped all season that perhaps having all the aces up my sleeve would be helpful to this bunch. In that moment, it was sort of the ultimate "us" against "them". It was my way of saying—"I never doubted you, so from top to bottom, we just need to believe that we have what it takes to perform at our highest level right now."

Funny how easy it is to recall a time when maybe a motivational strategy worked, but I have way more stories of when I got it wrong. I think we would agree that internal or intrinsic motivation is what we really hope for. A team full of highly motivated individuals who compete with self-confidence and are able to stay in the moment don't need a lot of motivational coaching.

You may be mentally reviewing some recent motivational tactics you have attempted. My advice is have fun with this. Start with this scale, which might provide a little comic relief.

## Pep Talk Scale

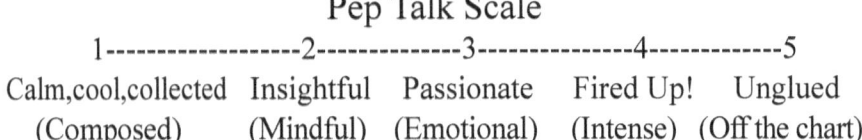

You get the picture. A wide variety of emotional levels can be deployed. A quick search on the topic of "pep talk effectiveness" should provide caution to us as coaches. Since individuals will respond differently—in some cases, our fiery speeches can throw them off. Get to know your people, and make note of what seems to make them tick.

Challenge your team members, and at the same time ask them what their greatest obstacle to success is. Remember, as you learned in Chapter Six (page 69), pep talks don't always have to come from you. I hesitate to add this, so will simply offer a challenging question. How would your team use the scale above to rate your last "post-game loss conversation" with the team? A calm discussion or a tirade? You will grow in this area, if you pay attention to the outcome of your inspirational approaches—not just pre-game, but post-game as well.

Allow the challenges and adversity that come your way to serve as motivators. If ever there was a situation where setting the example as the leader is critical, it would be in working through failure and failings. In professional golf, one statistical category is labeled "bounce back". The top bounce back golfers are those who follow an above par score on a hole, with a below par score on the very next hole. Those competitors have learned to keep looking AHEAD at the next opportunity for success. They use the gap available that begins when they walk off the green, and ends when the they step onto the next tee box. That gap opportunity is about mindset—"I will bounce back" is the self-talk of steely competitors. Leaders need to bounce back often, because adversity will come around quite frequently. Be motivated to make the necessary corrections, and come back stronger than ever.

# Chapter Eleven Review

- If adversity is defined as "difficulties" or "misfortune", then leadership provides a generous helping.
- Take note when your internal radar (antennae) is shouting that "something" is wrong.
- Consider both the mirror and window as you confront adversity.
- Expect the unexpected.
- Allow the challenges and adversity that come your way to serve as motivators.

1 – Do you have a favorite cliché, quote or story that inspires you in overcoming adversity?

2 – When you see the phrase, "Who would ever have thought….?", what comes to mind?

3 – Reflect on your most recent unexpected challenge. How would you rate your response to it?

4 – Remind yourself (below) of a time when you were highly motivated.

5 – Who do you go to for a pep talk?

# Chapter 12 – Vision:
# What is the End You Have in Mind?

Reverse engineering. I tend to start at the end of things and work my way back—I guess it is the visionary part of me. This process helps me to have a clear view of what I want something to look like, and then consider what it will take to make that picture a reality. I recall a first-year player we had who I was confident could develop into a dominant attacker. I knew it would take time, and I sensed she lacked self-confidence. During practice sessions, I often would move around the court to provide feedback as drills and competitive games ensued. A few times during her first season, when she was out of the action on the sideline, and standing apart from others, I paused behind her and quietly shared this thought, "You have no idea how good you are going to be".

I would continue on my way, hopeful that planting that thought in her mind, would help her grab that vision for herself. I repeated that a handful of times that season, and not surprisingly her game got better every year. She was pretty unstoppable in her final season. There was no magic involved, as she needed to commit to technical training, and test her developing abilities against strong competition for a few seasons in order to "get to" the level I certainly envisioned.

A former student recently reminded me of a class activity he found impactful. In discussing vision, the students were challenged to write a letter to their "future" self. Should you take this on, perhaps remind your future self about the non-negotiables in your foundation, and issue a challenge to routinely look for blind spots. The letter could include leadership development objectives like, "Become more of an independent thinker".

As leaders, gaining insight into the importance of perspective as it relates to vision is critical. As an athletic administrator, I secretly appreciated the most assertive coaches who seemed to have an endless list of budget impact requests. They forced me to say no, yet I couldn't fault the vision they had for their program. In the many years I found myself in that same situation, I certainly tried to prioritize my appeals when it came time to submit budget requests. I got some no's that were not unexpected. My approach was to continue to ask each year, with a note that captured a thought about past requests. "Please note this is my fourth year requesting the following..."

As I gained experience, I also realized and began to appreciate more fully, that while I had my program to tend to, I was also part of something larger than that. My colleagues and friends shared the same challenges and duties as they labored up and down the hallway from my office. I began to think more globally when it came time to provide input or cast a vote in a department meeting.

As your career moves forward, give thought to the big picture. When you are in the trenches gaining experience, and on your way to eventually serving in a leadership role, take the time to see what lies AHEAD. Place yourself in the shoes of an administrator as you plan a one-on-one meeting with a significant request you plan to make. Sure, you need to advocate strongly for your piece of the pie, so do your homework, and show up prepared. Perhaps one aspect of that preparation is to ask yourself, how would you see that request, if you were on the other side of the desk? Don't be so singularly focused on your part of the company that you undervalue others. A future promotion may land you suddenly in oversight of several other branches of the company, supervising personnel who you used to compete with for budget allocations.

For those of you just starting out as a leader, some of this may be a bit too much for where you are at. So let me pump the brakes, and keep it simple.

---

**There are times, when those you are leading are just looking for something—anything from you.**

---

Leaders need to answer the "call to action", but have wisdom in doing so. When success is achieved in some way, we "get to" acknowledge the collective work of the team. We can get a bit too focused on how people see us and our accomplishments, when in fact, we need to stay focused on what we are doing.

In *Ego is the Enemy*, author Ryan Holiday mentions "To be or to do?" which is the title of an early chapter. The author provides some background on Colonel John Boyd, a USAF fighter pilot "legend". Boyd became the lead instructor at an elite Fighter Weapons School. He became known for sharing straightforward messages of inspiration with those he trained. His challenge to "aspiring" pilots centered on the idea of determining whether you are more interested in being somebody or doing something. Holiday suggests to the reader, "The choice Boyd puts in front of us comes down to purpose. What is your purpose? What are you here to do?"[17] Those are two great questions for all of us as leaders to consider.

There are many books about leaders having a vision, and most feature examples of heroes, and heroic efforts. Some examples, are just the opposite—women and men straining against the odds and opposition. Despite the obstacles, those individuals who—stood in the gap—persist, and inspire us. Some like Martin Luther King Jr. to this day, give me chills when I hear his message and his powerful voice: "I have a dream".

The balance of looking AHEAD, but not getting AHEAD of yourself looms out there for each leader. I've heard variations of the following banquet, "honoree tribute" used many times, and I think it is appropriate here in relating to this topic. The speaker in referring to the one being recognized shares, "They say there are three kinds of leaders. First, those who watch what is happening". Looking for a little levity, they continue with, "The second is the group who say, what the heck is happening?" Following a pause for effect, the closing thought is, "The third type of leader is like our honoree, someone who makes things happen!"

Take that with you in developing your leadership approach. Take action, bold action when needed. I would also share one related piece of career advice. You may have already made a career move or two, and if not, you likely will. Some around you will caution you as you make those decisions about having regret. Visionary leaders make those decisions, and in making a new commitment, determine right there and then to have a forward-thinking mindset. What good will regret ever do you once your letter of resignation has been received? Move AHEAD. Look AHEAD. Make it a great move. You are the one in the gap between the previous job, and the new one. You get to . . . write that story! If your most recent move is your first with leadership responsibility, I am hopeful this book becomes a helpful resource in some way.

# Goal Setting

What one word from the 21st Olympic Games hosted in 1976 in Montreal comes to mind when you hear the name Nadia Comaneci? Perfection. Until I did a little review of her performances, I did not realize that when she attained a perfect 10.0, the scoreboard could only display 1.0. The technology at that time wasn't programmed to handle her unheard of—perfect score. Comaneci's performance rivals Bob Beamon's eye-popping result when he moved the world long jump record more than a foot in an historic leap in the '68 Games.

As leaders, that idea of continuous improvement will translate into an effort towards achieving perfection—maybe that would be a good way of looking at striving. With such an elusive goal, becoming a perfectionist could be a mistake—but straining towards what is AHEAD does result in some monumental moments. The photo finish for sprinters depicts this for the viewer in a powerful way. Canadian, R. Tait MacKenzie, was a childhood friend of James Naismith—the inventor of basketball. MacKenzie was an athlete, educator, soldier, physician, and a sculptor. He was commissioned by the American Olympic Committee to produce a sports medallion for the 1912 Stockholm Games. This medallion—called the "Joy of Effort"—won the King's Medal from the King of Sweden.[18] Let me encourage you leaders—find joy in your effort.

The original Olympic motto is represented by three Latin words, *citius, altius, fortius*. The translation (swifter, higher, stronger) represents the ideal and standard of these historic games. Notice the emphasis is not on swiftest, highest, or strongest. As leaders we can relate to this. Perhaps the best word to drive us towards achievement is "better". Isn't that what a growth mindset is about?

## Let's just get "better".

The established culture in our volleyball program included having a championship mindset. The phrase I used was "chasing championships". I always felt this was realistic for our program. Yet the chasing part—I hoped—kept the emphasis on the process, and daily collective effort with the ultimate goal of lining up late in the season with a championship on the line. Like any team, we were going to win some and lose some, but the only way to capture a championship is to get there. That was the goal.

Isn't that essentially the essence of goal setting? We establish the goal (and best to write it down and keep it visible by the way), and then we set off to reach it. Most leaders will have plenty of goals for themselves, but we also need to have them for our team members. Most coaches and teams value and really enjoy the pre-season goal setting process. The optimism in pre-season is unreal. Athletes have not yet lost a contest or an event, and they can fill a page with individual goals they have for the season. One of my former students, now a highly successful coach, talks about "Wanting to bottle that enthusiasm for the whole season". Team activities to agree upon goals for the team are often unrealistic. It would not be unusual to see "undefeated" on the list of considerations. That perfection notion is stubborn isn't it?

In discussing goal setting with one business owner, the approach has often been to start with a long-term goal, then work backwards. If having "x" in sales by year 5 is the long-term goal, her advice is to then set interim, short-term time-specific goals that as you achieve them, lead you closer to achieving that "x".

I'd like to challenge your thinking today, just as my own thinking was challenged years ago by a very experienced coach. She reminded me that effective goal setting takes time, and lots of it. Once players have established their goals for the season, by mid-season at the latest, another discussion between a coach and that player is needed. During this exchange, ask this simple question, "Where are you now with your season goals?" Re-visiting individual goals with your players can be another positive step in relationship building, and allows for revisions if necessary. Collective team goals are usually identified as part of team building activities during pre-season. Often, as the season progresses, the team needs the help of the coach in re-assessing, and re-positioning some goals. Your team needs to know where they stand and what is still on the line for your program related to championship opportunities.

First year players don't always know how play-off selection occurs, and I believe they need to understand. Maybe consider letting your seniors share this information. It was evident to me in most cases, that my seniors had play-offs on their minds a lot. They wanted to go out in style.

Finally, there is one more step for you to consider—the importance of scheduling one final round of individual meetings soon after the season ends. I recognize and remember the ever-present time demands I felt as a coach, and these meetings take a lot of time to complete.

I discovered there was no better way to send my players into their off-season than to look BEHIND before looking AHEAD. With some guidance, these final meetings allowed players to grow in terms of setting realistic, achievable, and measurable goals.

In summary, by systematically promoting the idea of a series of goal setting meetings with individual players, you are building in a lot of one-on-one communication. This process allows you to show how much you care about your players on an individual basis. You also have a great stepping off point established that you can refer to the following season. By re-visiting team goals, it is more likely that you can keep everyone on the same page throughout the season. I like both of those factors.

Allow me to share an example of re-framing that occurred to me related to team goal setting during the global pandemic. More than one coach asked me for my thoughts, on how to approach an upcoming season that had been officially cancelled. This really stumped me, and for good reason. I had no experience coaching a team where the season schedule was fully cancelled. I truly wanted to help coaches during this time, and it took a long while before I finally felt I had something to contribute. I began to share with coaches, "Listen, this might be the only undefeated season you ever have. Take full advantage of this one season where there will be no individual player meetings where you field objections over playing time. This will be the only season of your career, where you will have no long days on a bus, getting home long after bedtime, when your team lost a contest at the very end of the competition. Use this season to build your team cohesion like never before".

How will you make goal setting a team sport in your organization? Your annual review and employee evaluation process is a good opener. Comparing the performance review you have completed on someone with the self-evaluation they were required to submit is a great place to start, and certainly will allow for some good one-on-one discussion.

# Get To . . . The Banquet

"Get to...the banquet". For those who accepted their selection to our team, this was the expected commitment. Our end of the season banquet always highlighted and celebrated our seniors, and rightly so. In most cases, these student-athletes had remained steadfast and loyal for four years, and they deserved to have their moment to shine in front of peers and family. We always included a brief moment of public recognition of our seniors at the final home match of the regular season, but the banquet represented the final day together for any particular team. The main part of our celebration was hearing from those seniors, as each of them in turn shared with the group some reflections from their journey.

These players were in the "gap" from their first pre-season practice, right up to the last chance they got to wear their jersey. Grit, resiliency, loyalty, and commitment brings them to that banquet year after year. Determination, discipline, and diligence are the types of words that I worked into my comments to describe our "guests of honor". I'm guessing in their next to last banquet, they each started to think AHEAD to the following year. Soon enough, it would be their time to be honored. It's not easy saying good-bye, but the banquet certainly provided a great send-off.

Not every coach at every level can finish with a banquet. At the high school and collegiate levels, championship level Spring season sports may be competing long after graduation day and the close of the school year. Establishing a tradition of how you will end those seasons is important. One of my coaching friends always scheduled one last practice following the final match of the year. What a neat idea—a practice that truly would be just for fun, friendship, and fellowship.

We all like good endings. We grow up hearing "happily ever after" fairy tale stories, and when we need to watch a feel-good movie, look no further than the Hallmark channel. Years ago, I often listened to Paul Harvey's radio stories. He set them up before a commercial break, and then returned with his famous line, "And now. . . the rest of the story". Generally, these were good endings.

Do you remember a time when a book you were reading created so much uncertainty and/or curiosity that you flipped to the last few pages to see how it was going to end? We aren't able to do that with an athletic team. We need to show up, and see what happens. In fact, unless your team wins a state championship or NCAA title, most seasons end with a loss. The confetti will fall for the WNBA or Stanley Cup champions, and of course it is fun to watch a team erupt with joy when the final buzzer goes off. Instead of a stinging loss concluding the chase for a championship, a banquet tradition allows for a good ending for every season. As leaders we can be thinking about annual traditions to recognize accomplishments, long tenure, or just celebrate. What are the natural conclusions associated with your company or organization? When do your team members come together and celebrate?

When you name the end that you have in mind for a project, initiative, or fundraising effort, how is that celebrated? As a leader, how do you handle the well-earned vacations of your employees once they punch out on their last work day before a highly anticipated trip? Do they "get to" enjoy that time fully, or must they remain available 24/7? How about you? Is the culture you have shaped make you indispensable, even when you plan a vacation?

There are so many ways to look AHEAD, to map out a trip or exciting adventure. The planning and preparation help build up the anticipation, and despite unexpected delays or detours, we generally reach our destination. Looking AHEAD to something positive is only natural, but not at the expense of losing sight of what is right in front of us. I think most experienced leaders are asked for insight on the secret to success. I commented on this back in Chapter Two, but it bears repeating. My standard response developed over time is, "There is no secret to success. Show up every day and do an honest day's work, then repeat that the next day."

Beyond the banquet, our teams had many "ending" opportunities to capitalize on, so we took the time to determine how the conclusion of each rally, each set, and each match would be handled. To enhance cohesion, we established routines and protocols to follow. These rules of the road helped immensely when tensions were high, and emotions strong, especially when the scoreboard did not go our way. Each time-out concluded with a cheer, and at the conclusion of each match after participating in the handshake line, our team gathered on the endline for a brief two minutes. We handled debriefs on our performance the next day once statistics and video had been studied, but in those two minutes we came together. There was something symbolic in starting and finishing each match on the endline. For each new performance, the players were reminded that once again they "get to" step on that court and battle their way back to the post-match endline with the result they had in mind.

When our team was asked to volunteer and participate in service projects, our veteran players did a great job setting a good example in responding. Their willingness to help others was evident with an attitude that communicated, "we don't have to" do this, we "get to" do this. That is the true spirit of volunteering, and a wonderful way to introduce or create a discussion about servant leadership.

Our attitudes will be expressed in so many ways and in so many situations as we lead others. Effective leaders come in many forms. We hear the statement from time to time, "If you love what you do, you will never work a day in your life". As leaders, we "get to" set the tone, and we "get to" set the example for others to follow.

Looking for a place to start? How about a new emphasis on gratitude by mixing in some extra thank yous, or establishing new traditions to accomplish that? When I was little, I stayed after school every day. Now, hold on a minute, you need to understand that is different than being kept after school every day. In my elementary school years, I was a P.K., a principal's kid. Dad was my ride home.

No matter how long it took him to wrap up in his office, he often took me for a walk down the hallways on the way out. He ducked his head into every classroom, where a devoted teacher was still in her room, setting things up for the next day or correcting a pile of papers. Dad would smile and thank them, and continue to do so with everyone he encountered on his exit tour.

The custodians by this time were moving all the desks and chairs to one side of the room, and sweeping the rooms, and each one got a thank you. On any first encounters, he would introduce me to that staff person. I was taught to shake hands firmly, look that person in the eye, and say something like, "It's nice to meet you." Generally, Dad would then describe—in front of the employee—the key elements of that person's job. He would mention how late they would work that day, and how important their role was behind the scenes for the success of the school. I grew up observing a culture where gratitude was expressed daily.

When I discovered in my early years of coaching in Rhode Island, just how much work went into running a home tournament, I instituted a tradition with our players. At the conclusion of each away tournament, our players were expected to seek out the home coach and offer an expression of thanks for inviting us and for the work they put into the event. I'd like to think that, even though this was a "prescribed" thank you, our players delivered it sincerely. I often wondered if it might have been the first "thank you" that coach had heard for quite some time.

When I left that institution, somewhere along the way, I let that tradition go. I was humbly reminded of that at the conclusion of a home tournament where my program was competing against that same team, including several I had coached. Following the closing awards ceremonies, I was starting to work through the post-event checklist. I looked up and a line of athletes from my previous school, appeared in front of me. One after the other shook my hand and said, "Coach, thanks for having us."

So, what do you "get to" do today? The scale below provides one way of looking at the phrase "to do". How can we change our mindset and avoid being driven and controlled by our daily lists of tasks to complete? Do these descriptors help with that?

## To Do Scale

1------------------2------------------3----------------4-------------5

| Don't want to do | Have to do | Need to do | Want to do | Get to do |

Perhaps, you should create another scale with options like: to do, to not do, must do, should do, could do, will do—perhaps even throw a "do-over" in there. Hopefully, one of these approaches will be helpful to you. "Get to" is a powerful little phrase to consider and apply to the culture you are providing leadership for. It's a phrase that fits in nicely with forward thinking. What we get "to do" is AHEAD, it's in front of us—that is the final arrow in the $A^2B^2$ Leadership framework.

A leader who has a vision for those under his wing will be remembered for that. He will also be remembered for stepping up to support those same team members when life gets difficult. Be sure to take care of the people you have been given charge of. Every person in your workforce is going to face loss, and emotional pain in their personal lives. You will know about some of that, but many of those struggles will be kept appropriately from you. However, there will be days, if you are close enough to the action, where you sense something is wrong. Hopefully, you will learn to be sensitive to that, and respond with encouragement.

Visionary leaders get comfortable with regularly looking AHEAD, but without getting AHEAD of themselves. Experiences in leadership, will help us make the connections needed between knowledge, understanding, and wisdom. Solomon is remembered for his desire to receive a discerning heart, and we benefit from his writings and exhortations to "Get wisdom, get understanding" (Proverbs 4:5a).[19] As you lead, keep learning. Gain knowledge and understanding and apply it to your work. The opportunity to do that will be readily available to you.

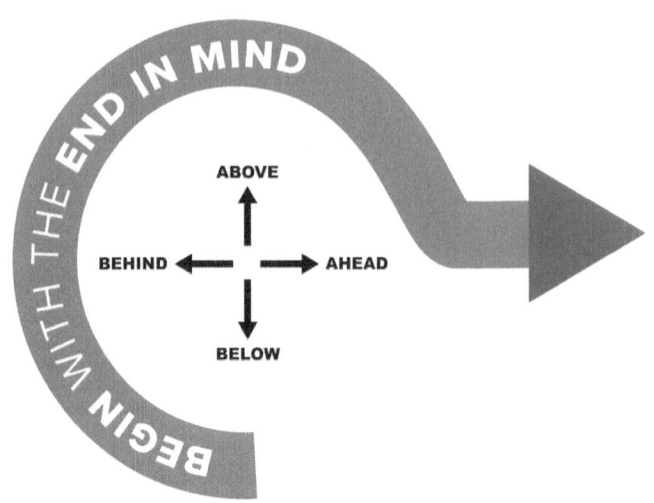

The hope is that the figure above, and all that I chose to share in discussing this leadership framework will be especially helpful to *aspiring, developing, and emerging* leaders. A primary aim of this book is to help you think things through, and gain greater insight for the daily challenges awaiting you.

As you encounter those challenges, opportunities, and decisions:

RELY on the strong foundation of your Integrity Switch.  **BELOW**

REFLECT often and learn lessons from your progress  **BEHIND** as a leader.

REFRAME - think for yourself when your leadership antennae goes off.  **ABOVE**

RESOLVE again and again to pursue your vision, ➡ **AHEAD** and adapt as needed.

Finally, REMEMBER every day, how neat it is that you "get to" lead.

## Chapter Twelve Review

- There are times, when those you are leading are just looking for something—anything from you.
- Perhaps the best word to drive us towards achievement is "better". Let's just get better.
- Looking AHEAD to something positive is only natural, but not at the expense of losing sight of what is right in front of us.
- Visionary leaders get comfortable with regularly looking AHEAD, but without getting AHEAD of themselves.

1 – Describe someone who had a vision for you, or helped you discover what you are passionate about or a career path you have pursued, or intend to pursue.

Consider sending a handwritten thank you note to them. What a nice keepsake for them as a reminder of their impact.

2 – Remind yourself of a goal setting process you participated in, and how it worked out for you. (could be as simple as your last set of New Year resolutions).

3 – Do you have something AHEAD that represents a good ending for your team? (an annual event, a celebration, an awards system, etc.)

4 – LETTER TO MY FUTURE SELF. Determine the time frame for when you will re-open it. For *developing* leaders, a 3 to 5-year time frame might be profitable. For *experienced* leaders, perhaps you could suggest this assignment for someone you are mentoring.

5 – What do you "get to" do?

# Afterword

Check my high school yearbook, and the only distinction there attributed to me by my classmates was "Most Helpful". It was not until I retired from coaching, some 35 years later, that perhaps I could appreciate that designation. I was often confronted in 2011 by family, colleagues, and friends always asking the same, simple question, "Do you miss coaching?" Eventually, I answered the question by simply referencing my primary core value—helping others. My typical response was, "I certainly miss my players, and all involved—but I'm still helping students in my new role of training future leaders."

What I valued most in all those years of building teams and guiding athletes through those 40+ seasons, was "helping" them. Helping them achieve their dreams. Helping them technically to improve. And . . . helping them in that lofty goal of using the lessons learned to navigate life challenges long after their final team banquet was well back in the rear-view mirror. Suspecting in some cases, and clearly recognizing in others, where I may not have been particularly helpful to those I coached or mentored as future coaches always stayed with me. Perhaps as a leader, you can relate to that? I have tried to use the lessons learned from those reflections, and especially the failures, to get better as a leader, and to help other leaders.

# Now Here Scale

1---------------2------------------3------------------4---------------5

Nowhere    Somewhere    Are we there yet?    Almost there   Now here

I've been saving this scale for just the right place. Since we find ourselves "now here", this must be the spot. In leadership challenges, we can feel lost or at least at a loss for our next move. We plunge in and we make progress. Initially, it feels as if we are *nowhere* near a solution, in fact, we may not be making headway initially. Then, we start to get *somewhere*. We address issues, but will wonder, *"Are we there yet?"* The closer we get to resolution, we realize we are *almost there*. Most of the time, closure comes. Tasks and objectives, like finishing this book, bring us to this place. We are *now here*. The chapters, content, stories, and many challenging questions have come your way. You stood *in the gap* between starting and finishing. Do I hope I have impacted your thoughts on framing topics and challenges? Yes. A wish for you is that you may start *re-framing* situations, obstacles, and opportunities in leadership as well.

Bring *blind spot* consideration and the *integrity switch* challenge along with you. One last prompt from Dad, written on an index card I still have—Be steady, heady, and ready! Make sure that your leadership gets defined just the way you hope, and that your impact over time becomes evident to all. This will make your effort all worthwhile. It's time to move on. The time for a leader never really changes. Why? Because, the time is always now! Remember that.

# Endnotes

1.     The Holy Bible (Good News Translation).

2.     Covey, S. (1989) The 7 *Habits of Highly Effective People.*
Simon & Schuster, New York, NY.

3.     Peters, T. and Austin, N. (1985) *A Passion for Excellence.*
New York: Random House.

4.     Wooden, J. & Carty, J. (2003) *Coach Wooden One-on-One.*
Regal Books from Gospel Light, Ventura, CA.

5.     DiCicco, T., Hacker, C. & Salzberg, C. (2002) *Catch Them
Being Good: Everything you need to know about coaching girls.*
1st published by Viking Penguin, a member of Penguin Putnam, Inc.
New York, NY.

6.     Depree, M. (2004) *Leadership Is An Art.* Crown Business:
New York (Crown Business, an imprint of the Crown Publishing
Group, a division of Random House LLC, A Penguin Random House
Company, NY).

7.     Martens, R. (2012) *Coaching Successfully.* (4th ed.). Human
Kinetics: Champaign, IL.

8.     Scott, S. (2002) *Fierce Conversations: Achieving Success in
Work & in Life, One Conversation at a Time.* Viking / Published by
the Penguin Group, New York.

9.     Maxwell, J. (2003) *Attitude 101: What every leader needs to
know.* Thomas Nelson, Inc., Publishers. Nashville, TN.

10.    Sawtell, W.R. (1983) *Coach and his boys.* 1983, W.R. Sawtell.

11.    Dearing, J. (Aug/Sept, 2012). *Follow The Leader: Beyond Captain Selection.* Coaching Volleyball, 8-11.

12.    Merriam-Webster Dictionary. Definition of: "think outside the box." Merriam-Webster.com. 2024. https://www.merriam-webster.com (15 Feb 2024).

13.    Greenleaf, R. (1977). *Servant Leadership: A Journey into the Nature of Legitimate Power and Greatness.* Paulist Press, Mahwah, NJ.

14.    Sanborn, M. (2004). *Fred Factor: How Passion in Your Work and Life Can Turn the Ordinary into the Extraordinary.* Crown Currency, New York.

15.    RUDY (film, 1993). TriStar Pictures.

16.    TIME Magazine (January, 1999). *The End of the World?*

17.    Holiday, R. (2016). *The Ego is the Enemy.* Portfolio/ Penguin New York.

18.    MacKenzie, R Tait. *The Joy of Effort.* https://en.wikipedia.org/wiki/R._Tait_McKenzie,  Last retrieved Feb 15, 2024.

19.    The Holy Bible (NIV).

# Leadership Scales

### Introduction
### Best Way Scale

1-------------2-------------3-------------4-------------5

| Easy | Safe | Fair | Right | Best |
|------|------|------|-------|------|
| Way  | Way  | Way  | Way   | Way  |

### Chapter One
### Integrity Switch Scale

1---------------2-------------3-----------------4-----------------5

Broken        Off        On        Low Beams        High Beams

### Chapter Two
### The Trust Scale

1---------------2-------------3-----------------4-----------------5

Broken    Compromised    Intact    Evident    Trustworthy

### Chapter Three
### Conversation Scale

1---------------2-------------3-----------------4-----------------5

Guarded        Polite        Candid        Real        Fierce

## Chapter Four
## Failure Response Scale

1----------------2------------------3-----------------4---------------5

Oblivious    Ignore    Recognize    Address    Unpack

## Chapter Five
## Keep / Stop / Start Feedback Scale

1----------------2------------------3-----------------4---------------5

Stop    Pause    Keep    Modify    Start

## Chapter Six
## Strengthen Strengths Scale

1--------------2------------------3---------------4---------------5

Find    Validate    Exercise    Utilize    Maximize

(Identity)

## Chapter Seven
## Uncommon Sense Scale

1----------------2------------------3-----------------4----------------5

Nonsense    No    Common    Makes    Uncommon

    Sense    Sense    Sense    Sense

## Chapter Eight
### Impact of Change Scale

```
1---------------2-------------------3-----------------4--------------5
Smooth        Choppy           Moderate       Turbulence       Gale
Sailing                         Waves                      Force Winds
```

## Chapter Nine
### Team Commitment Scale

```
1---------------2-------------------3-----------------4--------------5
Out         Toe in water        1 foot in        In           All In
                                1 foot out
```

## Chapter Ten
### Success Scale

```
1---------------2-------------------3-----------------4--------------5
I won't       I can't         I think I can      I can         I will
```

## Chapter Eleven
### Pep Talk Scale

```
1------------------2--------------3---------------4------------5
Calm,cool,collected Insightful  Passionate   Fired Up!    Unglued
(Composed)        (Mindful)   (Emotional)   (Intense)  (Off the chart)
```

## Chapter Twelve
## To Do Scale

1------------------2------------------3----------------4--------------5

| Don't want | Have | Need | Want | Get |
|------------|------|------|------|-----|
| to do | to do | to do | to do | to do |

## Afterword
## Now Here Scale

1--------------2------------------3------------------4--------------5

Nowhere    Somewhere    Are we there yet?   Almost there   Now here

# Index

**D**

**E**

# I

# J

# K

# L

# M

# N

# O

# P

# Q

# R

# S

## About the author

Joel Dearing coached women's and men's volleyball over a span of 30 years and a total of 40 seasons (Roger Williams University 1981-89), then (Springfield from 1989-2010). Dearing had a career record of 899-384, coached 10 All-Americans and his Springfield men's team finished the 1996 season #1 and undefeated in NCAA Division III. During his career, he conducted volleyball clinics in Argentina, Aruba, Bermuda, China, and Ireland.

Author of *Volleyball Fundamentals* (1st and 2nd editions) *and The Untold Story of William G. Morgan – Inventor of Volleyball*, Coach "D" also served for over 25 years on the USA Volleyball CADRE (National Faculty). He owned and operated Dearing Volleyball School, Inc. from 1991-2017, and launched Dearing Leadership, LLC. in 2018.

He was honored in 2013 by the International Volleyball Hall of Fame as the Mintonette Medallion of Merit Award honoree, and in 2019 by the Fellowship of Christian Athletes as an inductee into the FCA Hall of Champions. He was inducted into the Springfield College Athletic Hall of Fame (2015), the Roger Williams University Athletic Hall of Fame (2019), and the American Volleyball Coaches Association (AVCA) Hall of Fame (2019). In addition to his coaching career, Dearing served as Director of Athletics at Roger Williams University and Graduate Program Director for athletic administration at Springfield College.